AAT
ASSESSMENT KIT

Foundation Unit 3

Ledger Balances and Initial Trial Balance

In this June 2001 edition

- Extra practice activities have been included in the Kit

- The Kit is up to date for developments in the subject as at 1 June 2001

FOR 2001 AND 2002 ASSESSMENTS

BPP Publishing
June 2001

First edition 2000
Second edition June 2001

ISBN 0 7517 6402 7 (Previous edition 0 7517 6232 6)

British Library Cataloguing-in-Publication Data
A catalogue record for this book
is available from the British Library

Published by

BPP Publishing Limited
Aldine House, Aldine Place
London W12 8AW

www.bpp.com

Printed in England by W M Print
45 – 47 Frederick Street
Walsall
West Midlands WS2 9NE

All our rights reserved. No part of this publication may be reproduced, stored in a retrieval system or transmitted, in any form or by any means, electronic, mechanical, photocopying, recording or otherwise, without the prior written permission of BPP Publishing Limited.

We are grateful to the Lead Body for Accounting for permission to reproduce extracts from the Standards of Competence for Accounting.

©

BPP Publishing Limited
2001

CONTENTS

	Page
Activity Checklist/Index	(v)
How to use this Assessment Kit	
Aims of this Assessment Kit	(viii)
Recommended approach to this Assessment Kit	(viii)
Lecturers' Resource Pack activities	(ix)
Central assessment technique	(x)
Unit 3 Standards of Competence	
The structure of the Standards for Unit 3	(xii)
Unit 3 Preparing Ledger Balances and an Initial Trial Balance	(xii)
Assessment strategy	(xv)

	Activities	Answers
Practice activities	3	161

> Practice activities are short activities directly related to the actual content of the BPP Interactive Text. They are graded pre-assessment and assessment.

Practice devolved assessments	29	179

> Practice devolved assessments consist of a number of tasks covering certain areas of the Standards of Competence but are not full assessments.

Trial run devolved assessment	63	193

> Trial run devolved assessments are of similar scope to full simulations.

AAT sample simulation	79	203
Trial run central assessments	101	217

> Trial run central assessments are full central assessments providing practice for the AAT's actual central assessment

AAT specimen central assessment	129	231
December 2000 central assessment	143	239

Contents

	Activities	Answers
Lecturers' resource pack activities	247	-

> Lecturers' resource pack activities are practice activities and assessments for lecturers to set in class or for homework. The answers are given in the BPP Lecturers' Resource Pack.

ORDER FORM

REVIEW FORM & FREE PRIZE DRAW

Activity Checklist/Index

		Activities	Answers	Done
PRACTICE ACTIVITIES				
Chapter 1 Revision of basic bookkeeping				
1	Stock or asset	3	161	☐
2	Advice note	3	161	☐
3	Redecoration	3	161	☐
4	Remittance advice	3	161	☐
5	Business documentation	3	161	☐
Chapter 2 Recording, summarising and posting transactions				
6	Which ledger?	4	162	☐
7	Delivery van	4	162	☐
8	Classifying accounts	4	162	☐
9	Entries	4	162	☐
10	Whereabouts	5	162	☐
11	Main ledger entries	5	162	☐
Chapter 3 From ledger accounts to initial trial balance				
12	Batch processing	6	163	☐
13	Calculating VAT	6	163	☐
14	More VAT	6	163	☐
15	Correcting errors	6	163	☐
Chapter 4 Bank reconciliations				
16	Standing orders	7	164	☐
17	Journals	7	164	☐
18	Bank statement entries	7	164	☐
19	Update	7	165	☐
20	Compare	8	165	☐
21	Balance	9	166	☐
Chapter 5 Stock and bad debts				
22	Stock control account 1	11	167	☐
23	Stock control account 2	11	167	☐
24	Cash control 1	11	167	☐
25	Cash control 2	12	167	☐
26	Cash control 3	12	167	☐
27	Wages 1	13	168	☐
28	Wages 2	13	168	☐
29	Wages 3	14	168	☐
30	Stock record card 1	15	169	☐
31	Stock record card 2	16	170	☐
Chapter 6 Debtors control account				
32	Recording transaction	18	171	☐
33	Errors cause a difference	18	171	☐
34	Set off	18	171	☐
35	Three reasons	18	171	☐
36	Debtors control account reconciliation	19	171	☐

Activity Checklist/Index

		Activities	Answers	Done
Chapter 7 Creditors control account				
37	Balance of CCA	21	173	☐
38	Another set off	21	173	☐
39	Transactions with suppliers	21	173	☐
40	More differences	22	173	☐
41	Creditors control account reconciliation	22	173	☐
Chapter 8 Filing				
42	Documents for trial balance	24	175	☐
43	Filing correspondence	24	175	☐
44	Storage	24	175	☐
45	Creditors' accounts	24	175	☐
46	Accounts personnel	24	175	☐
PRACTICE DEVOLVED ASSESSMENTS				
1	Comart Supplies Ltd	29	179	☐
2	Chang Fashions Ltd	39	182	☐
3	MEL Motor Factors	47	185	☐
4	Music World	53	188	☐
TRIAL RUN DEVOLVED ASSESSMENT				
1	TS Stationery	63	193	☐
AAT SAMPLE SIMULATION		79	203	☐
TRIAL RUN CENTRAL ASSESSMENTS				
1	JWL Ltd	101	217	☐
2	Hathaway Design & Print	115	223	☐
AAT SPECIMEN CENTRAL ASSESSMENT		129	231	☐
DECEMBER 2000 CENTRAL ASSESSMENT		143	239	☐

Activity Checklist/Index

Activities Answers Done

LECTURERS' RESOURCE PACK ACTIVITIES

LECTURERS' PRACTICE ACTIVITIES

Chapter 1 Revision of basic bookkeeping

1	Revenue	250	-	☐
2	Classify	250	-	☐
3	Appropriate	250	-	☐

Chapter 2 Recording, summarising and posting transactions

4	Imprest	251	-	☐
5	Primary records	251	-	☐

Chapter 3 From ledger accounts to initial trial balance

6	Advantages	252	-	☐
7	Manufacturer	252	-	☐
8	Children's clothes	252	-	☐

Chapter 4 Bank reconciliations

9	Debit or credit	253	-	☐
10	Fill in	253	-	☐
11	Not accepted	254	-	☐

Chapter 5 Stock and bad debts

12	Bankrupt	255	-	☐
13	Stock control	255	-	☐

Chapter 6 Debtors control account

14	Reasons	256	-	☐
15	Contra	256	-	☐

Chapter 7 Creditors control account

16	File, record or field	257	-	☐
17	One reason	257	-	☐

Chapter 8 Filing

18	Codes	258	-	☐
19	Methods	258	-	☐
20	Documents	258	-	☐

LECTURERS' PRACTICE DEVOLVED ASSESSMENTS

1	Future electrical	261	-	☐
2	Hairdressing supplies	267	-	☐

LECTURERS' PRACTICE CENTRAL ASSESSMENT

279 - ☐

How to use this Assessment Kit

HOW TO USE THIS ASSESSMENT KIT

Aims of this Assessment Kit

> To provide the knowledge and practice to help you succeed in the central and devolved assessment for Technician Unit 3 *Preparing Ledger Balances and an Initial Trial Balance*.

To pass the central and devolved assessment you need a thorough understanding in all areas covered by the standards of competence. Devolved assessment may be in the workplace, although it is more likely to take the form of simulation. Either way, you need practical experience of relevant tasks.

> To tie in with the other components of the BPP Effective Study Package to ensure you have the best possible chance of success.

Interactive Text
This covers all you need to know for the central and devolved assessment for Unit 3 *Preparing Ledger Balances and an Initial Trial Balance*. Icons clearly mark key areas of the text. Numerous activities throughout the text help you practise what you have just learnt.

Central and Devolved Assessment Kit
When you have understood and practised the material in the Interactive Text, you will have the knowledge and experience to tackle the Central and Devolved Assessment Kit for Unit 3 *Preparing Ledger Balances and an Initial Trial Balance*. This aims to get you through the central assessment and the devolved assessment, whether in the form of the AAT simulation or in the workplace.

Recommended approach to this Assessment Kit

(a) To achieve competence in all units you need to be able to do **everything** specified by the standards. Study the Interactive Text very carefully and do not skip any of it.

(b) Learning is an **active** process. Do **all** the activities as you work through the Interactive Text so you can be sure you really understand what you have read.

(c) After you have covered the material in the Interactive Text, work through this **Assessment Kit**.

(d) Try the **Practice Activities**. These are linked into each chapter of the Interactive Text, and are designed to reinforce your learning and consolidate the practice that you have had doing the activities in the Interactive Text. Depending on their difficulty, they are graded as Pre-assessment or Assessment.

(e) Then attempt the **Practice Devolved Assessments**. These are designed to test your competence in certain key areas of the Standards of Competence and will give you practice at completing a number of tasks based upon the same data.

(f) Next do the **Trial Run Devolved Assessment**. It is designed to cover the areas you might see when you do a full devolved assessment.

(g) Next try the AAT's **Sample Simulation** which gives you the clearest idea of what a full devolved assessment will be like.

(h) Then try the Trial Run Central Assessments. They will give you a good idea of what you will meet in the 'real thing'.

(i) **Try the AAT's Specimen Central Assessment and the December 2000 Central Assessment**. It is probably best to leave these until the last stage of your revision, and then attempt them as 'mocks' under 'exam conditions'. This will help you develop techniques in approaching the assessment and allocating time correctly. For further guidance on this, please see Central Assessment Technique on Page (x).

Remember this is a **practical** course.

(a) Try to relate the material to your experience in the workplace or any other work experience you may have had.

(b) Try to make as many links as you can to your study of the other units at this level.

Lecturers' Resource Pack activities

At the back of this Kit we have included a number of chapter-linked activities without answers. We have also included two practice devolved assessments and a trial run central assessment without answers. The answers for this section are in the BPP Lecturers' Resource Pack for this Unit.

Central Assessment Technique

CENTRAL ASSESSMENT TECHNIQUE

Passing central assessments at this level is half about having the knowledge, and half about doing yourself full justice on the day. You must have the right **technique**.

The day of the central assessment

1 Set at least one **alarm** (or get an alarm call) for a morning central assessment

2 Have **something to eat** but beware of eating too much; you may feel sleepy if your system is digesting a large meal

3 Allow plenty of **time to get to where you are sitting the central assessment**; have your route worked out in advance and listen to news bulletins to check for potential travel problems

4 **Don't forget** pens, pencils, rulers, erasers

5 Put **new batteries** into your calculator and take a spare set (or a spare calculator)

6 **Avoid discussion** about the central assessment with other candidates outside the venue

Technique in the central assessment

1 *Read the instructions (the 'rubric') on the front of the paper carefully*

   Check that the format of the paper hasn't changed. It is surprising how often assessors' reports remark on the number of students who attempt too few questions. Make sure that you are planning to answer the **right number of questions.**

2 *Select questions carefully*

   Read through the paper once - don't forget that you are given 15 minutes' reading time - then quickly jot down key points against each question in a second read through. Select those questions where you could latch on to 'what the question is about' - but remember to check carefully that you have got the right end of the stick before putting pen to paper. Use your 15 minutes' reading time wisely.

3 *Plan your attack carefully*

   Consider the **order** in which you are going to tackle questions. It is a good idea to start with your best question to boost your morale and get some easy marks 'in the bag'.

4 *Check the time allocation for each section of the paper*

   Time allocations are given for each section of the paper. When the time for a section is up, you must go on to the next section. Going even one minute over the time allowed brings you a lot closer to failure.

5 *Read the question carefully and plan your answer*

   Read through the question again very carefully when you come to answer it. Plan your answer to ensure that you **keep to the point**. Two minutes of planning plus eight minutes of writing is virtually certain to earn you more marks than ten minutes of writing.

6 *Produce relevant answers*

Particularly with written answers, make sure you **answer the question set**, and not the question you would have preferred to have been set.

7 *Gain the easy marks*

Include the obvious if it answers the question, and don't try to produce the perfect answer.

Don't get bogged down in small parts of questions. If you find a part of a question difficult, get on with the rest of the question. If you are having problems with something, the chances are that everyone else is too.

8 *Produce an answer in the correct format*

The assessor will state *in the requirements* the format in which the question should be answered, for example in a report or memorandum.

9 *Follow the assessor's instructions*

You will annoy the assessor if you ignore him or her. The **assessor will state** whether he or she wishes you to 'discuss', 'comment', 'evaluate' or 'recommend'.

10 *Lay out your numerical computations and use workings correctly*

Make sure the layout fits the **type of question** and is in a style the assessor likes.

Show all your **workings** clearly and explain what they mean. Cross reference them to your answer. This will help the assessor to follow your method (this is of particular importance where there may be several possible answers).

11 *Present a tidy paper*

You are a professional, and it should show in the **presentation of your work**. Students are penalised for poor presentation and so you should make sure that you write legibly, label diagrams clearly and lay out your work neatly. Markers of scripts each have hundreds of papers to mark; a badly written scrawl is unlikely to receive the same attention as a neat and well laid out paper.

12 *Stay until the end of the central assessment*

Use any spare time **checking and rechecking** your script.

13 *Don't worry if you feel you have performed badly in the central assessment*

It is more than likely that the other candidates will have found the assessment difficult too. Don't forget that there is a competitive element in these assessments. As soon as you get up to leave the venue, **forget** that central assessment and think about the next - or, if it is the last one, celebrate!

14 *Don't discuss a central assessment with other candidates*

This is particularly the case if you **still have other central assessments to sit**. Even if you have finished, you should put it out of your mind until the day of the results. Forget about assessments and relax!

UNIT 3 STANDARDS OF COMPETENCE

The structure of the Standards for Unit 3

The Unit commences with a statement of the **knowledge and understanding** which underpin competence in the Unit's elements.

The Unit of Competence is then divided into **elements of competence** describing activities which the individual should be able to perform.

Each element includes:

(a) A set of **performance criteria**. This defines what constitutes competent performance.

(b) A **range statement**. This defines the situations, contexts, methods etc in which competence should be displayed.

(c) **Evidence requirements**. These state that competence must be demonstrated consistently, over an appropriate time scale with evidence of performance being provided from the appropriate sources.

(d) **Sources of evidence**. These are suggestions of ways in which you can find evidence to demonstrate that competence. These fall under the headings: 'observed performance; work produced by the candidate; authenticated testimonies from relevant witnesses; personal account of competence; other sources of evidence.'

The elements of competence for Unit 3 *Preparing Ledger Balances and an Initial Trial Balance* are set out below. Knowledge and understanding required for the unit as a whole are listed first, followed by the performance criteria and range statements for each element.

Unit 3: Preparing Ledger Balances and an Initial Trial Balance

What is the unit about?

This unit relates to the internal checks involved in an organisation's accounting processes. The first element is primarily concerned with comparing individual items on the bank statement with entries in the cash book, and identifying any discrepancies. This involves recording details from the relevant primary documentation, including cheque counterfoils, paying-in slips and standing order schedules, in the cash book, and calculating the totals and balances of receipts and payments. The element also requires the individual to identify any discrepancies, such as uncertainty in coding and differences identified by the matching process.

The second element requires the individual to total the relevant accounts and to reconcile the control accounts, such as debtors, creditors, cash and wages and salaries, with the totals of the balance in the ledgers. The individual is also required to resolve or refer any discrepancies and to ensure security and confidentiality.

The third element involves identifying and obtaining the information required for an initial trial balance from the computer system, relevant files, ledgers, colleagues and the appropriate managers and accountants. The element requires the individual to prepare the trial balance in the appropriate format up to the draft stage, seeking advice from the relevant people where necessary.

Unit 3 Standards of Competence

Knowledge and understanding

The business environment

- Types of business transactions and the documents involved (Elements 3.1 & 3.2)
- General bank services and operation of bank clearing system (Element 3.1)
- Function and form of banking documentation (Element 3.1)

Accounting methods

- Operation of manual and computerised accounting systems (Elements 3.1, 3.2 & 3.3)
- Identification of different types of errors (Element 3.1)
- Relationship between the accounting system and the ledger (Elements 3.1 & 3.2)
- Methods of posting from primary records to ledger accounts (Element 3.2)
- Inter-relationship of accounts - double entry system (Elements 3.2 & 3.3)
- Use of journals (Elements 3.2 & 3.3)
- Methods of closing off ledger accounts (Element 3.2)
- Reconciling control accounts with memorandum accounts (Element 3.2)
- Function and form of the trial balance (Element 3.3)

The organisation

- Relevant understanding of the organisation's accounting systems and administrative systems and procedures (Elements 3.1, 3.2 & 3.3)
- The nature of the organisation's business transactions (Elements 3.1, 3.2 & 3.3)
- Organisational procedures for filing source information (Elements 3.1, 3.2 & 3.3)

Element 3.1 Balance bank transactions

Performance criteria

1. Details from the relevant primary documentation are recorded in the cash book
2. Totals and balances of receipts and payments are correctly calculated
3. Individual items on the bank statement and in the cash book are compared for accuracy
4. Discrepancies are identified and referred to the appropriate person

Range statement

1. Primary documentation: credit transfer and standing order schedules
2. Discrepancies: uncertainty in coding; differences identified by the matching process

Unit 3 Standards of Competence

Element 3.2 Prepare ledger balances and control accounts

Performance criteria

1 Relevant accounts are totalled
2 Control accounts are reconciled with the totals of the balance in the subsidiary ledger, where appropriate
3 Authorised adjustments are correctly processed and documented
4 Discrepancies arising from the reconciliation of control accounts are either resolved or referred to the appropriate person
5 Documentation is stored securely and in line with the organisation's confidentiality requirements

Range statement

1 Ledgers: main ledger; sub ledger; integrated ledger
2 Control accounts: stock; debtors; creditors; cash; wages and salaries
3 Adjustments: to correct errors; to write off bad debts

Element 3.3 Draft an initial trial balance

Performance criteria

1 Information required for the initial trial balance is identified and obtained from the relevant sources
2 Relevant people are asked for advice when the necessary information is not available
3 The draft initial trial balance is prepared in line with the organisation's policies and procedures
4 Discrepancies are identified in the balancing process and referred to the appropriate person

Range statement

1 Sources: colleagues; computer system; files; manager; accountant; ledger
2 Discrepancies: incorrect double entries; missing entries; wrong calculations

ASSESSMENT STRATEGY

This unit is assessed by **devolved assessment** and **central assessment**.

Devolved assessment

Devolved assessment is a means of collecting evidence of your ability to **carry out practical activities** and to **operate effectively in the conditions of the workplace** to the standards required. Evidence may be collected at your place of work, or at an Approved Assessment Centre by means of simulations of workplace activity, or by a combination of these methods.

If the Approved Assessment Centre is a **workplace**, you may be observed carrying out accounting activities as part of your normal work routine. You should collect documentary evidence of the work you have done, or contributed to, in an **accounting portfolio**. Evidence collected in a portfolio can be assessed in addition to observed performance or where it is not possible to assess by observation.

Where the Approved Assessment Centre is a **college or training organisation**, devolved assessment will be by means of a combination of the following.

- Documentary evidence of activities carried out at the workplace, collected by you in an **accounting portfolio**.

- Realistic **simulations** of workplace activities. These simulations may take the form of case studies and in-tray exercises and involve the use of primary documents and reference sources.

- **Projects and assignments** designed to assess the Standards of Competence.

If you are unable to provide workplace evidence you will be able to complete the assessment requirements by the alternative methods listed above.

Possible assessment methods

Where possible, evidence should be collected in the workplace, but this may not be a practical prospect for you. Equally, where workplace evidence can be gathered it may not cover all elements. The AAT regards performance evidence from simulations, case studies, projects and assignments as an acceptable substitute for performance at work, provided that they are based on the Standards and, as far as possible, on workplace practice.

There are a number of methods of assessing accounting competence. The list below is not exhaustive, nor is it prescriptive. Some methods have limited applicability, but others are capable of being expanded to provide challenging tests of competence.

Assessment Strategy

Assessment method	Suitable for assessing
Performance of an accounting task either in the workplace or by simulation: eg preparing and processing documents, posting entries, making adjustments, balancing, calculating, analysing information etc by manual or computerised processes	**Basic task competence.** Adding supplementary oral questioning may help to draw out underpinning knowledge and understanding and highlight your ability to deal with contingencies and unexpected occurrences
General case studies. These are broader than simulations. They include more background information about the system and business environment	Ability to **analyse a system** and suggest ways of modifying it. It could take the form of a written report, with or without the addition of oral or written questions
Accounting problems/cases: eg a list of balances that require adjustments and the preparation of final accounts	Understanding of the **general principles of accounting** as applied to a particular case or topic
Preparation of flowcharts/diagrams. To illustrate an actual (or simulated) accounting procedure	**Understanding of the logic** behind a procedure, of controls, and of relationships between departments and procedures. Questions on the flow chart or diagram can provide evidence of underpinning knowledge and understanding
Interpretation of accounting information from an actual or simulated situation. The assessment could include non-financial information and written or oral questioning	**Interpretative competence**
Preparation of written reports on an actual or simulated situation	**Written communication skills**
Analysis of critical incidents, problems encountered, achievements	Your ability to handle **contingencies**
Listing of likely errors eg preparing a list of the main types of errors likely to occur in an actual or simulated procedure	Appreciation of the range of **contingencies** likely to be encountered. Oral or written questioning would be a useful supplement to the list
Outlining the organisation's policies, guidelines and regulations	Performance criteria relating to these aspects of competence. It also provides evidence of competence in **researching information**
Objective tests and short-answer questions	**Specific knowledge**
In-tray exercises	Your **task-management ability** as well as technical competence
Supervisors' reports	**General job competence,** personal effectiveness, reliability, accuracy, and time management. Reports need to be related specifically to the Standards of Competence

Assessment Strategy

Assessment method	Suitable for assessing
Analysis of work logbooks/diaries	**Personal effectiveness**, time management etc. It may usefully be supplemented with oral questioning
Oral questioning	**Knowledge and understanding** across the range of competence including organisational procedures, methods of dealing with unusual cases, contingencies and so on. It is often used in conjunction with other methods

Central Assessment

A central assessment is a means of collecting evidence that you have the **essential knowledge and understanding** which underpins competence. It is also a means of collecting evidence across the **range of contexts** for the standards, and of your ability to **transfer skills**, knowledge and understanding to different situations. Thus, although central assessments contain practical tests linked to the performance criteria, they also focus on the underpinning knowledge and understanding. You should in addition expect each central assessment to contain tasks taken from across a broad range of the standards.

Format of Central Assessment

With the introduction of the Revised Standards for the Level 2 NVQ/SVQ in Accounting, there will be a single Central Assessment which will be based on Unit 3 *Preparing Ledger Balances and an Initial Trial Balance*.

The Central Assessment will be in two sections and of three hours duration. It will be based on an organisation which operates a manual accounting system consisting of a main ledger and subsidiary ledgers. The main ledger has in the past been known as the general (nominal) ledger and the subsidiary ledgers as the sales and purchase ledgers. Candidates can assume that the control accounts will be contained in the main (general) ledger forming part of the double entry. The individual accounts of debtors and creditors will be in the subsidiary ledgers and will therefore be regarded as memorandum accounts.

Section 1 will always ask candidates to enter opening balances into accounts, record transactions from primary accounting records, balance off accounts and complete an initial trial balance.

The primary accounting records given could be a selection from sales and sales returns day books **or** purchases and purchase returns day books, cash book and journal. In the past feedback from centres and candidates has indicated that it is confusing to include both sales and purchase day books as primary accounting records. As there is only enough room/time available to feature one subsidiary ledger, and in response to this feedback, the Central Assessment at Foundation level will give extracts from the sales/sales returns day books **or** purchase/purchase returns day books, but not both.

The candidate will be asked to transfer the balances calculated in the first part of section 1 to the trial balance, and then to transfer the remaining balances from a given list.

Assessment Strategy

Candidates should total the debit and credit columns of the trial balance, which should be equal.

Candidates are advised to take 90 minutes to complete section 1. Whilst the aim should be to produce a trial balance with the total of the debit and credit columns equal, candidates should not sacrifice checking time, or time allocated for section 2, in an attempt to discover the reason for an imbalance. On completion of both sections, if the candidates is still within the three hours time allowed, it is at this point that they should revisit section 1 and make further checks for accuracy.

Section 2 will always contain a mixture of 10 questions and tasks, some of which will be short-answer, and some requiring a longer response. Typical examples of the tasks which a candidate can expect are, balance reconciliation, debtors/creditors reconciliation, journal entries and completion of banking and business documentation.

Further guidance

The following guidance is taken from the AAT's Newsletter *Summing Up*.

The first Central Assessment for the revised Foundation Level has now been held. Candidates' performance was excellent.

One of the issues which arose was that candidates need to ensure that they have mastered the technique of balancing accounts before they undertake this Unit. There have also been queries received regarding the inclusion of law (such as contracts, offers and acceptance) in the Central Assessment. The law of contract is part of the knowledge and understanding in Units 1 and 2 (Recording Income and Receipts (RIR) and Making and Recording Payments (MRP) and as such will not be included in the Central Assessment. However candidates can expect to be assessed on business documentation as this is included in the knowledge and understanding of the first three units of the revised Foundation. Indeed, questions on this issue are included in the Specimen Central Assessment. The function and form of banking documentation is also a feature of Unit 3 and as such could be centrally assessed.

There have also been queries received regarding where specific issues are assessable in the first three units of the Standards – notably balances carried down, control accounts (including debtors control accounts) and aged debtors analysis. To clarify – balances carried down are specifically referred to in the knowledge and understanding of Unit 3 (ITB) but also implied in the knowledge and understanding of Unit 1 (RIR) and Unit 2 (MRP). Reconciling control accounts are primarily an issue included in Units 3, Preparing Ledger Balances and an Initial Trial Balance (ITB), but as Units 1 and 2 (RIR and MRP) call for entries into the ledgers, the debtors and creditors control accounts will be featured in these units. Aged debtors analysis is assessable under RIR and is specifically mentioned in the range of Element 1.1 as a source document for communicating with customers.

Centres have also asked about the inclusion of bank reconciliation statements at this Stage of the Accounting NVQ/SVQ. Bank reconciliation *statements* are not included in the revised Foundation. However, bank reconciliation *activities* are – candidates will be required to undertake the matching process and recognise the cause of the difference in the balance on the bank statement and the balance in the cash book once updated.

(xviii)

However, the candidate will only be asked to list the differences and not to produce a bank reconciliation statement.

Summary

IN

- Matching cash book and bank statement
- Debtors/creditors reconciliation
- Short answer questions
- Journal entries
- Completion of banking and business documentation

OUT

- **Contract law** (although it could be included in a portfolio)

- **Discounts other than processing aspects,** ie transfer to cash book, although students will need to know it for Unit 2

- **General VAT principles,** although the double entry will be tested

- **Legal relationship of banker and customer**

- **Legal aspects of cheques including crossing and endorsement** although this may come up indirectly as part of banking documentation

- **Credit card procedures.** Again students may have to complete a paying-in slip as part of 'business documentation'

- **Age analysis report,** which may, however, be used in the portfolio

- **Bank reconciliation statements,** although the activity will still be featured

(xx)

＃ Practice activities

Practice activities

1 Revision of basic bookkeeping

1 STOCK OR ASSET   Pre-assessment

Comart Supplies Ltd has recently purchased five ITC computers. Would the purchase be regarded as capital expenditure or revenue expenditure if:

(a) The computers are to be used for data processing by the company?

Capital / Revenue

(b) The computers are to be held as stock for sale to customers?

Capital / Revenue

2 ADVICE NOTE   Pre-assessment

An advice note is a document sent to a customer advising the customer or acknowledging that an order has been received.

True / False

3 REDECORATION   Assessment

Mary Chang has decided that some of the offices are looking rather shabby. She arranges for the walls to be redecorated and for the purchase of some new office furniture.

(a) Is the cost of the redecoration capital or revenue expenditure?

Capital / Revenue

(b) Is the cost of the new office furniture capital or revenue expenditure?

Capital / Revenue

4 REMITTANCE ADVICE   Pre-assessment

A remittance advice is a document sent by a supplier to a customer to advise the customer that goods ordered have been sent off to the customer.

True / False

5 BUSINESS DOCUMENTATION   Assessment

What would be the appropriate document to be used in each of the following cases?

(a) MEL Motor Factors Ltd sends out a document to a credit customer on a monthly basis summarising the transactions that have taken place and showing the amount owed by the customer.

(b) MEL Motor Factors Ltd sends out a document to a credit customer in order to correct an error where the customer has been overcharged on an invoice.

(c) MEL Motor Factors Ltd wishes to buy certain goods from a supplier and sends a document requesting that those goods should be supplied.

Practice activities

2 Recording, summarising and posting transactions

6 WHICH LEDGER?   Pre-assessment

Would the following accounts be found in the main ledger, the creditors or the debtor ledger?

(a) Debtors control account
(b) Sales account
(c) Shop fitting repairs

7 DELIVERY VAN   Pre-assessment

MEL Motor Factors is about to purchase a new delivery van costing £7,821.

(a) Would it normally be appropriate to make a purchase of this kind out of petty cash?

(b) Explain, briefly, the reason for your answer.

8 CLASSIFYING ACCOUNTS   Pre-assessment

Classify the balance on each of the following general ledger accounts as an asset, a liability, an expense or revenue.

(a) Advertising
(b) Discount received
(c) Debtors control
(d) VAT
(e) Postage and stationery

9 ENTRIES   Assessment

The credit balance of £92 (including VAT @ 17.5%) on the debtor's account of Euro Hair Style Ltd on 1 March arose because of an overcharge on a sales invoice which was subsequently corrected. However, Euro Hair Style has paid the original amount shown on the invoice.

(a) What document would have been sent to Euro Hair Style when the overcharge was corrected?

(b) Show the entries in the general ledger accounts, including amounts, made when this document was issued.

Debit   *Credit*
£   £
_____   _____
_____   _____

Practice activities

10 WHEREABOUTS *Pre-assessment*

Would the following accounts be found in the main ledger, the purchase ledger or the sales ledger?

(a) Exotic Blooms Ltd (a credit supplier) ....

(b) Salaries and wages ....

(c) Motor vehicles ....

11 MAIN LEDGER ENTRIES *Assessment*

What book-keeping entries would be required in the **main ledger** to correct the following error?

A credit note for £160 plus £28 VAT issued to a customer has been treated as if it were a credit note received.

Debit	Amount £	Credit	Amount £
....	....	....	....
....	....	....	....
....	....	....	....
....	....	....	....
....	....	....	....
....	....	....	....

Practice activities

3 From ledger accounts to initial trial balance

> **Tutorial note.** For extensive practice on this topic use the devolved and central assessments in this kit.

12   BATCH PROCESSING   Pre-assessment

Batch processing is a system whereby transactions are processed as and when they arise in order to keep the ledgers totally up to date.

True / False

13   CALCULATING VAT   Pre-assessment

For the quarter ended 31 March 20X5, sales amounted to £1,821,250 inclusive of VAT. On 31 March, the balance of the VAT account was £26,250 credit. Calculate the total of the taxable purchases made during the quarter *exclusive* of VAT.

14   MORE VAT   Pre-assessment

Music World Ltd purchases 80 CDs at £7.50 each plus VAT. These are then all sold to a customer for a total of £846 inclusive of VAT. What sum will be owing to HM Customs & Excise in respect of this purchase and sale?

15   CORRECTING ERRORS   Assessment

What double entry would you make in the general ledger if you had to correct the following errors?

(a) An invoice received from Smith's Electrics Ltd had been entered in the relevant day book but the VAT element of £14 had been omitted.

(b) The £98 total of the discounts allowed column in the cash book had been debited to discounts received.

(c) A credit note issued to a customer for £23 plus £4 VAT had been posted to the general ledger as a credit note received.

Practice activities

4 Bank reconciliations

16   STANDING ORDERS   Pre-assessment

Today's date is 1 May 20X1 and you are currently checking the month end balances on the ledger accounts as at 30 April 20X1. You have in front of you the automated payments schedule and note the following standing orders that have not yet been entered into the accounting records.

25th of each month	Standing order	District Council (rates)	£140
28th of each month	Standing order	Friendly Insurance Company	£80
30th of each month	Standing order	Telephone Corporation	£125

What is the double entry for each of these standing orders?

17   JOURNALS   Pre-assessment

When the bank statement is received by your business for the month ending 30 June 20X0 three items appear on the bank statement which are not in the cash book:

14 June	Bank giro credit receipt	Johnson & Co (a debtor)	£1,245
30 June	Direct debit	English Gas Co	£330
30 June	Bank charges		£40

Prepare journal entries for each of these amounts showing the double entry required in the main ledger and a brief narrative explaining the entries.

18   BANK STATEMENT ENTRIES   Pre-assessment

When looking at the bank statement for your business for the month of January 20X1 you note the following entries.

		Debit £	*Credit* £
14 January	CR Cheque paid in	156.50	
20 January	DR Returned cheque		156.50

What do these entries in the bank statement mean and what further action should be taken?

19   UPDATE   Assessment

Given below is the cash book for your business for the month of June 20X1.

CASH BOOK						
RECEIPTS			**PAYMENTS**			
Date	*Detail*	*£*	*Date*	*Detail*	*Cheque no*	*£*
1 June	Bal b/d	572	5 June	J Taylor	013647	334
8 June	Hardy & Co	493	16 June	K Filter	013648	127
12 June	T Roberts	525	22 June	B Gas	013649	200
18 June	D Smith	617	28 June	Wages	BACS	940
25 June	Garnet Bros	369	29 June	D Perez	013650	317

Practice activities

You are also given the bank statement for the same period.

```
CENTRAL BANK
43, Main Street
York
YK2 3PT

CHEQUE ACCOUNT     Lenten Trading     Account number 19785682

SHEET 0141
                                  Paid out    Paid in    Balance
                                     £           £          £

1 June    Opening balance                                  572
4 June    Bank giro credit - A Hammond           136       708
11 June   Cheque 013647            334                     374
12 June   Credit                                 493       867
16 June   Credit                                 525     1,392
18 June   DD - Telephone Company   146                   1,246
22 June   Credit                                 617     1,863
27 June   Cheque 013649            200                   1,663
28 June   BACS                     940                     723
30 June   Bank interest                             11     734
```

Tasks

(a) Check the bank statement and the cash book and update the cash book for any missing entries.

(b) Balance the amended cash book.

(c) Explain what the reason for cheque numbers 013648 and 013650 not appearing on the bank statement might be.

20 COMPARE   Assessment

Given below is the cash book for your business for the month of February 20X1.

CASH BOOK						
RECEIPTS			**PAYMENTS**			
Date	Detail	£	Date	Detail	Cheque no	£
2 Feb	Davis & Co	183	1 Feb	Balance b/d		306
7 Feb	A Thomas	179	4 Feb	J L Pedro	000351	169
14 Feb	K Sinders	146	11 Feb	P Gecko	000352	104
21 Feb	H Harvey	162	15 Feb	F Dimpner	000353	217
27 Feb	A Watts	180	23 Feb	O Roup	000354	258

Practice activities

You are also given the bank statement for the month:

EASTERN BANK
20/24 Miles Square
Huddersfield
LD3 5FS

CHEQUE ACCOUNT L Arnold Account number 29785643

SHEET 0141

		Paid out £	Paid in £	Balance £	
1 February	Opening balance			306	O/D
8 Feb	Credit		183	123	O/D
12 Feb	Credit		179	56	
15 Feb	SO - Telephone	65			
	000352	104		113	O/D
20 Feb	Credit		146	33	
	000353	217		184	O/D
24 Feb	DD - Electricity	30		214	O/D
26 Feb	Credit		162		
	000351	169		221	O/D
28 Feb	Interest	15		236	O/D

Tasks

(a) Compare the bank statement to the cash book and amend the cash book accordingly.

(b) Find the closing balance on the amended cash book and state whether this would be a debit or a credit balance in the trial balance.

(c) Make a note of the reasons why the closing balance on the bank statement still does not agree with the amended balance on the cash book.

21 BALANCE   Assessment

Given below is the cash book for your organisation for the month of January 20X1.

CASH BOOK						
RECEIPTS			**PAYMENTS**			
Date	Detail	£	Date	Detail	Cheque no	£
1 Jan	Balance b/d	1,035	2 Jan	O J Trading	02475	368
2 Jan	Filter Bros	115	4 Jan	K D Partners	02476	463
8 Jan	Headway Ltd	640	7 Jan	L T Engineers	02477	874
15 Jan	Letterhead Ltd	409	14 Jan	R Trent	02478	315
22 Jan	Leaden Partners	265	20 Jan	I Rain	02479	85
			25 Jan	TDC	SO	150
			28 Jan	Wages	02480	490

Practice activities

You are also given the bank statement for the month.

```
WESTERN BANK
Bank house
Leeds Road
Halifax
LD3 5FS
```

CHEQUE ACCOUNT   Frant & Co   Account number 43709436

SHEET 0276

Date	Details	Paid out £	Paid in £	Balance £
1 Jan	Opening balance			1,035
6 Jan	CR		115	
	CH 02475	368		782
12 Jan	CR		640	
	CH 02477	784		638
19 Jan	CR		409	1,047
20 Jan	BGC - T Elliot		161	
	CH 02478	315		893
23 Jan	CH 02476	463		430
25 Jan	SO - TDC	150		280
28 Jan	CR		265	
	Charges	10		535

Tasks

(a) Compare the cash book to the bank statement and amend the cash book appropriately.

(b) Balance the amended cash book.

(c) Note why the amended cash book balance does not agree with the bank statement balance at the end of January.

5 Stock and bad debts

22 STOCK CONTROL ACCOUNT 1   *Assessment*

STOCK CONTROL

Date	Details	£	Date	Details	£
1 March	Balance b/f	30,000			

This is the stock control account of Dinsdale Ltd. However, a recent physical stock check revealed goods in stock totalled £28,600. What may have caused this difference to occur?

23 STOCK CONTROL ACCOUNT 2   *Assessment*

STOCK CONTROL

Date	Details	£	Date	Details	£
1 March	Balance b/f	40,000			

This is the stock control account of Harold Ltd. However, a recent physical stock check revealed goods in stock totalled £44,200. What may have caused this difference to occur?

24 CASH CONTROL 1   *Assessment*

A petty cash control account is kept in the main (general) ledger of Coulthurst Ltd. The petty cash book is the subsidiary account. At the beginning of August there is a balance brought forward of £175.

During August £125 was spent from petty cash, and at the end of the month, £150 was put into the petty cash box from the bank.

Task

Enter these transactions into the petty cash control account below, showing clearly the balance carried down.

Practice activities

PETTY CASH CONTROL ACCOUNT

Date 20X1	Details	£	Date 20X1	Details	£

25   CASH CONTROL 2   Assessment

A petty cash control account is kept in the main (general) ledger of Wye Ltd. The petty cash book is the subsidiary account. At the beginning of June there is a balance brought forward of £150.

During June £100 was spent from petty cash, and at the end of the month, £200 was put into the petty cash box from the bank.

Task

Enter these transactions into the petty cash control account below, showing clearly the balance carried down.

PETTY CASH CONTROL ACCOUNT

Date 20X1	Details	£	Date 20X1	Details	£

26   CASH CONTROL 3   Assessment

A petty cash control account is kept in the main (general) ledger of Fabien Ltd. The petty cash book is the subsidiary account. At the beginning of April there is a balance brought forward of £232.

During April £210 was spent from petty cash, and at the end of the month, £220 was put into the petty cash box from the bank.

Task

Enter these transactions into the petty cash control account below, showing clearly the balance carried down.

PETTY CASH CONTROL ACCOUNT

Date 20X1	Details	£	Date 20X1	Details	£

27 WAGES 1   Assessment

Beta Ltd has extracted the following summary figures for wages and salaries for the month of September.

	£
Gross pay	6,000
Tax	1,100
Employees' NIC	400
Employer's NIC	600
Net pay	4,500

Task

Prepare and total the wages control account shown below.

WAGES CONTROL ACCOUNT

Date 20X0	Details	Amount £	Date 20X0	Details	Amount £

28 WAGES 2   Assessment

Gamma Ltd has extracted the following summary figures for wages and salaries for the month of September.

	£
Gross pay	12,000
Tax	2,200
Employees' NIC	800
Employer's NIC	1,200
Net pay	9,000

Practice activities

Task

Prepare and total the wages control account shown below.

Date 20X0	Details	Amount £	Date 20X0	Details	Amount £

29 WAGES 3   Assessment

Delta Ltd has extracted the following summary figures for wages and salaries for the month of September.

	£
Gross pay	30,000
Tax	5,500
Employees' NIC	2,000
Employer's NIC	3,000
Net pay	22,500

Task

Prepare and total the wages control account shown below.

Date 20X0	Details	Amount £	Date 20X0	Details	Amount £

30 STOCK RECORD CARD 1

Cook Ltd is a wholesaler of kitchen equipment for the catering trade. The year end is 31 December 20X0. A physical stock check has been carried out on product DW 156, the Multi-Kleen dishwasher. This revealed a stock of 278 items valued at £139,000.

Task

Complete the stock record card below and reconcile with the stock check figure. If there is a difference, make a note to your supervisor, saying what you think is the reason for this.

STOCK RECORD CARD – DW 156 MULTI-KLEEN DISHWASHER

Date 20X1	Details	In	Out	Quantity in stock	@ £500 per dishwasher £
1 Jan	Opening balance			348	174,000
1 Jan	Sales		20	328	164,000
4 Jan	Sales		40	288	144,000
6 Jan	Sales		100	188	94,000
7 Jan	Sales		30	158	79,000
11 Jan	Sales		40	118	59,000
12 Jan	Faulty		2	116	58,000
13 Jan	Sales		40	76	38,000
15 Jan	Sales		40	36	18,000
18 Jan	Receipt	200		236	118,000
20 Jan	Sales		20	216	108,000
22 Jan	Sales		10	206	103,000
25 Jan	Sales		30	176	88,000
26 Jan	Sales		40	136	68,000
28 Jan	Receipt	220		356	178,000
29 Jan	Sales		40	316	158,000
30 Jan	Sales		40	276	138,000

RECONCILIATION OF STOCK RECORD WITH PHYSICAL STOCK CHECK ON 31 JANUARY 20X1

	£
PHYSICAL STOCK CHECK 278 @ £500	139,000
STORES RECORD CARD QUANTITY (276 @ £500)	138,000
DIFFERENCE	1,000

Note to supervisor: The physical stock exceeds the stores record card quantity by 2 units (£1,000). The most likely reason is that the 2 faulty units noted on 12 January were written off the stores record card but are still physically present in the stockroom (awaiting return to supplier or disposal). Other possible explanations include a recording error on one of the sales or receipts entries, or a miscount during the physical stock check.

Practice activities

NOTE FOR SUPERVISOR

31 STOCK RECORD CARD 2   Assessment

Drinki-poo Ltd is a wholesaler of drinks machines to factories, offices and so on. The year end is 31 December 20X0. A physical stock check has been carried out on product RF 815, the 'Refresh-kwik' drinks machine. This revealed a stock of 417 items valued at £41,700.

Task

Complete the stock record card below and reconcile with the stock check figure. If there is a difference, make a note to your supervisor, saying what you think is the reason for this.

STOCK RECORD CARD – RF 815 REFRESH-KWIK

Date 20X1	Details	In	Out	Quantity in stock	@ £100 per machine £
1 Jan	Opening balance			522	52,200
1 Jan	Sales		30	492	49,200
4 Jan	Sales		60	432	43,200
6 Jan	Sales		150	282	28,200
7 Jan	Sales		45		
11 Jan	Sales		60		
12 Jan	Faulty		3		
13 Jan	Sales		60		
15 Jan	Sales		60		
18 Jan	Receipt	300			
20 Jan	Sales		30		
22 Jan	Sales		15		
25 Jan	Sales		45		
26 Jan	Sales		60		
28 Jan	Receipt	330			
29 Jan	Sales		60		
30 Jan	Sales		60		

RECONCILIATION OF STOCK RECORD WITH PHYSICAL STOCK CHECK ON 31 JANUARY 20X1

PHYSICAL STOCK CHECK 417 @ £100 _____

STORES RECORD CARD QUANTITY _____

DIFFERENCE _____

NOTE FOR SUPERVISOR

Practice activities

6 Debtors control account

32 RECORDING TRANSACTION   Assessment

Software has been sold on credit to Softsell Ltd, a new small business which is not registered for VAT. The invoice issued shows the cost of the software as £160 plus £28 VAT giving a total of £188. In recording the transaction which general ledger account(s) will be debited and which will be credited:

(a) In the books of Comart Computers Ltd?

Debit   *Credit*

………………………………………   ………………………………………

………………………………………   ………………………………………

(b) In the books of Softsell Ltd?

Debit   *Credit*

………………………………………   ………………………………………

………………………………………   ………………………………………

33 ERRORS CAUSE A DIFFERENCE   Pre-assessment

Would the following errors cause a difference to occur between the balance of the debtors control account and the total of the balances in the sales ledger?

(a) The total column of the sales day book was overcast by £100.

Yes / No

(b) In error H Lambert's account in the sales ledger was debited with £175 instead of M Lambert's account.

Yes / No

(c) An invoice for £76 was recorded in the sales day book as £67.

Yes / No

34 SET OFF   Assessment

Gift Box is both a supplier to and a customer of Bloomers Ltd. It has been agreed that a debt of £75 owing to Gift Box is to be set off against the balance of £300 owed by Gift Box.

What entries would be required in the main ledger to record this set off?

Debit   *Amount*   *Credit*   *Amount*
                         £   £

35 THREE REASONS   Pre-assessment

List three reasons for maintaining a debtors control account.

36 DEBTORS CONTROL ACCOUNT RECONCILIATION — Assessment

Using the summary activity shown below, complete the debtors control account showing clearly the balance carried down. Use the list of balances in the subsidiary (sales) ledger to reconcile this balance with the debtors control account. If there is an imbalance, make a note to your supervisor, suggesting where the error might be.

DEBTORS CONTROL ACCOUNT

Date 20X0	Details	Amount £	Date 20X0	Details	Amount £
1 Aug	Balance b/d	182,806	Aug	Sales returns	2,352
Aug	Sales	82,250	Aug	Discounts allowed	100
			Aug	Bank	73,648
			31 Aug	Balance c/d	188,956
		265,056			265,056
1 Sept	Balance b/d	188,956			

Details for reconciliation of the debtors control account

Summary of activity

	£
Opening balance at 1 August 20X0	182,806
Sales in August	82,250
Sales returns in August	2,352
Discounts allowed	100
Bank receipts from debtors	73,648

Balances in subsidiary (sales) ledger

	£
Tadman Ltd	29,142
Silvertown & Co	16,000
Talbot & Co	38,400
Hibbert Industries	46,036
Galactic Cleaners	30,034
Smith Ltd	(448)
Waldon & Co	28,896

RECONCILIATION OF DEBTORS CONTROL ACCOUNT
WITH SUBIDIARY (SALES) LEDGER
AT 31 AUGUST 20X0

	£
Closing balance of debtors control account	188,956
Total balance of accounts in subsidiary (sales) ledger	188,060
Imbalance	896

Practice activities

NOTE TO SUPERVISOR

Practice activities

7 Creditors control account

37 BALANCE OF CCA *Assessment*

Would the following errors cause a difference to occur between the balance of the creditors control account and the total of the balances in the purchases ledger?

(a) A creditor's account has been balanced off incorrectly.

Yes / No

(b) An invoice for £37 has been entered into the purchases day book as £39.

Yes / No

(c) An invoice has, in error, been omitted from the purchases day book.

Yes / No

38 ANOTHER SET OFF *Assessment*

Which account in the general ledger would you debit and which account in the general ledger would you credit in respect of the following.

(a) A set-off is to be made between Peter Allen's account in the sales ledger, which has a balance of £200, and his account in the purchases ledger, which has a balance of £450.

Debit   *Credit*

(b) The correction of an error where it has been found that an invoice for £36, received from Allied Brokers Ltd for insurance, has been entered in the various columns of the purchase day book as £63. (*Note.* Ignore VAT)

Debit   *Credit*

(c) The correction of an error where it has been discovered that the purchase of £10 of stationery has been debited to the purchases account.

Debit   *Credit*

39 TRANSACTIONS WITH SUPPLIERS *Pre-assessment*

Which general ledger account would be debited and which general ledger account credited in respect of each of the following transactions?

(a) Bought office furniture on credit from Crome Supplies Ltd.

(b) Credit note sent to Jean Crane & Co.

(c) Paid by cheque a credit account 'Alf Green & Sons' for last month's van repairs.

	Account to be debited	*Account to be credited*
(a)	_____	_____
(b)	_____	_____
(c)	_____	_____

Practice activities

40 MORE DIFFERENCES Pre-assessment

Would each of the following cause a difference between the totals of the main ledger debit and credit account balances at 31 March?

(a) A purchase invoice for £36 from P Smith was entered into P Short's account in the creditors ledger.

Yes / No

(b) A purchase invoice for £96 was not entered in the purchase day book.

Yes / No

(c) The total column of the purchase day book was undercast by £20.

Yes / No

(d) A purchase invoice from Short & Long for £42 for the goods for resale was entered as £24 in the purchase day book.

Yes / No

41 CREDITORS CONTROL ACCOUNT RECONCILIATION Assessment

A list of subsidiary ledger balances is shown below, together with a summary of activity in the month of August 20X0. Prepare a creditors control account as at 31 August 20X0, showing clearly the balance carried down. Reconcile this balance with the list of balances in the subsidiary (purchase) ledger.

Details for reconciliation of the creditors control account

Summary of activity

	£
Opening balance at 1 August 20X0	67,200
Purchases in August	63,450
Purchases returns in August	1,880
Discounts received	200
Bank payments to creditors	68,310

CREDITORS CONTROL ACCOUNT

Date	Details	Amount £	Date	Details	Amount £

Balances in subsidiary (purchases) ledger

	£
Donna Ltd	19,270
ABC Controls	14,100
Alex & John	11,750
S Rashid	9,400
XYZ Ltd	5,740

RECONCILIATION OF CREDITORS CONTROL ACCOUNT WITH SUBSIDIARY (PURCHASES) LEDGER AT 31 AUGUST 20X0

	£
Closing balance of creditors control account	
Total balance of accounts in subsidiary (purchases) ledger	_____
Imbalance	========

Practice activities

8 Filing

42 DOCUMENTS FOR TRIAL BALANCE — Assessment

When preparing a trial balance at the end of an accounting period there will be a number of documents and reconciliations that you will need to be able to find from the filing system. List the documents and reconciliations that you will need to access before completing the initial trial balance.

43 FILING CORRESPONDENCE — Pre-assessment

A small business has always filed its correspondence with customers and suppliers in date order. However as the business has grown the owner has found that it is harder to locate the correspondence required from the filing system.

Suggest a different method of filing that might make accessing the required correspondence easier.

44 STORAGE — Assessment

You are the bookkeeper in a small business and your office currently has no facility for storing the ledger accounts and other accounting records which you work on, including the wages book. These are all left on your desk when you are not in the office. You are to write a memo to the owner of the business expressing any concerns you may have about this system and suggesting ways of improving it. Today's date is 4 May 20X1.

45 CREDITORS' ACCOUNTS — Pre-assessment

The creditors' accounts in the subsidiary ledger, the purchases ledger, are filed in alphabetical order. In what order would the following creditors' accounts be filed?

- Smithson Ltd
- Sonic Partners
- Skelton Engineers
- Snipe Associates
- Spartan & Co
- Souter Finance

46 ACCOUNTS PERSONNEL — Assessment

A fairly large engineering business has the following accounts personnel.

- Chief accountant
- Cashier
- Petty cashier and bookkeeper
- Sales ledger clerk
- Purchases ledger clerk
- Wages clerk

With which of these personnel are you likely to find the following?

- Wages book

- Aged debtor analysis
- Creditors' accounts
- Bank statement
- Petty cash book
- Credit limits for customers
- Standing order schedule

Practice devolved assessments

Practice devolved assessment
1 Comart Supplies Ltd

Performance criteria

The following performance criteria are covered in this Devolved Assessment.

Element 3.1 Balance bank transactions

1 Details from the relevant primary documentation are recorded in the cash book

2 Totals and balances of receipts and payments are correctly calculated

3 Individual items on the bank statement and in the cash book are compared for accuracy

Element 3.2 Prepare ledger balances and control accounts

1 Relevant accounts are totalled

3 Authorised adjustments are correctly processed and documented

Notes on completing the Assessment

This Assessment is designed to test your ability to post transactions correctly to the cash book, including items on the bank statement, and to post and total the ledgers correctly.

You are allowed 2 hours to complete your work.

A high level of accuracy is required. Check your work carefully.

Correcting fluid may be used but should be used in moderation. Errors should be crossed out neatly and clearly. You should write in black ink and not in pencil.

A full answer to this Assessment is provided on page 179 of this Kit.

Do not turn to the answer until you have completed all parts of the Assessment.

Practice devolved assessments

Comart Supplies Ltd

The tasks and questions are based on the transactions of Comart Supplies Ltd. The company operates as a distributor of computer hardware, software and general consumables. It is located in Taunton in the UK.

The Managing Director is Paul Byrne and Louise Ford is the Accountant. You are employed as an Accounting Technician to assist Louise Ford.

DATA

The following transactions all occurred on 1 June 20X5 and have yet to be entered into the ledger system. VAT has been calculated to the nearest pound at a rate of 17.5% and you should continue to use this rate for any subsequent calculations. The bank statement was received on 2 June but contains transactions relating to 1 June.

Sales invoices issued

	Total £	VAT £	Net £
Computer Care Ltd	9,655	1,438	8,217
Bristol Micros	8,100	1,206	6,894
Silicon World	6,753	1,005	5,748
Other customers	16,891	2,516	14,375
	41,399	6,165	35,234

Purchases invoices received

	Total £	VAT £	Net £	Goods for resale £	Other items £
Smith Electronics Ltd	5,800	864	4,936	4,936	
ITC Computers Ltd	4,315	643	3,672	3,672	
Western Imports Ltd	11,266	1,678	9,588	9,588	
Other suppliers	13,148	1,958	11,190	10,090	1,100
	34,529	5,143	29,386	28,286	1,100

Analysis of other items purchased

	£
Telephones	264
Power and heating	626
Sundry expenses	210
	1,100

Credit note issued

	Total £	VAT £	Net £
Silicon World	193	29	164

Credit note received

	Total £	VAT £	Net £
ITC Computers Ltd	660	98	562

Journal entries

	Debit £	Credit £
Bad debts	493	
Debtors control account		493

Software City (included in the balance of other customers) debt written off.

Cheques issued

	£
ITC Computers	3,240
(In full repayment of a debt for £3,340)	

Cheques received

	£
Silicon World	6,024
(In full repayment of a debt for £6,275)	
Bristol Micros	7,687
Cash sales	1,645
(Inclusive of VAT of £245)	

Bank statement received

MIDWEST BANK PLC
Comart Supplies Ltd
Statement of Account

Account No: 80148762

Date	Details	Debit	Credit	Balance
1 June	Balance forward			3,465 o/d
1 June	Silicon World BGC		1,000	2,465 o/d
1 June	Loan Repayment TR	400		2,865 o/d
1 June	Cheque No. 302462	1,205		4,070 o/d

o/d Overdrawn   BGC Bank Giro Credit   TR Transfer

Practice devolved assessments

The following balances are available to you at the start of the day on 1 June 20X5.

	£
Customers	
Computer Care Ltd	45,261
Bristol Micros	32,310
Silicon World	29,873
Other customers	697,429
Suppliers	
Smith Electronics Ltd	23,572
ITC Computers Ltd	25,689
Western Imports Ltd	56,734
Other suppliers	502,173
Other	
Purchases	1,241,860
Sales	1,655,960
Purchases returns	7,798
Sales returns	8,346
Bank (credit balance)	4,670
Bank loan	16,200
Discount allowed	24,839
Discount received	18,628
Debtors control account	804,873
Creditors control account	608,168
VAT (credit balance)	69,173
Bad debts	NIL
Telephones	NIL
Power and heating	487
Sundry expenses	361
Various other debit balances - total	1,362,347
Various other credit balances - total	1,062,516

Practice devolved assessments

COMPLETE ALL THE FOLLOWING TASKS.

Task 1 Enter the opening balances into the following accounts:

Bank (cash book)
Bank loan
Debtors control account
Discount allowed
Discount received
Power and heating
Purchases
Sales
VAT
ITC Computers Ltd

These accounts can be found on pages 34 to 37.

Task 2 Using the data shown on pages 30 to 32, enter all relevant transactions into the accounts shown in Task 1. Please note that the cash book has been divided into two sections, one to record receipts and the other to record payments. When making entries in the cash book ensure that you complete the analysis columns (used to analyse amounts received and amounts paid) and that you include the bank giro credit and loan repayment shown in the bank statement on Page 31.

Task 3 Total the various columns of the cash book and clearly show the closing bank balance.

Task 4 Transfer any relevant sums from the cash book into the other accounts shown in Task 1.

Task 5 Balance off all the remaining accounts in which you have made entries.

Note You are not required to update any accounts other than those shown in Task 1.

Practice devolved assessments

GENERAL LEDGER

Receipts - cash book

Date	Details	Discounts £	Total received £	VAT £	Debtors £	Other £

Payments - cash book

Date	Details	Discounts £	Total paid £	VAT £	Creditors £	Other £

Bank loan

Date	Details	Amount £	Date	Details	Amount £

Debtors control account

Date	Details	Amount £	Date	Details	Amount £

Discount allowed

Date	Details	Amount £	Date	Details	Amount £

Discount received

Date	Details	Amount £	Date	Details	Amount £

Power and heating

Date	Details	Amount £	Date	Details	Amount £

Purchases

Date	Details	Amount £	Date	Details	Amount £

Sales

Date	Details	Amount £	Date	Details	Amount £

VAT

Date	Details	Amount £	Date	Details	Amount £

CREDITORS LEDGER

ITC Computers Ltd

Date	Details	Amount £	Date	Details	Amount £

Practice devolved assessment 2 Chang Fashions Ltd

Performance criteria

The following performance criteria are covered in this Devolved Assessment.

Element 3.2 Prepare ledger balances and control accounts

1   Relevant accounts are totalled

3   Authorised adjustments are correctly processed and documented

Element 3.3 Draft an initial trial balance

1   Information required for the initial trial balance is identified and obtained from the relevant sources

3   The draft initial trial balance is prepared in line with the organisation's policies and procedures

Notes on completing the Assessment

This Assessment is designed to test your ability to post transactions correctly to the ledgers and prepare an initial trial balance.

You are allowed 2 hours to complete your work.

A high level of accuracy is required. Check your work carefully.

Correcting fluid may be used but should be used in moderation. Errors should be crossed out neatly and clearly. You should write in black ink and not in pencil.

A full answer to this Assessment is provided on page 182 of this Kit.

Do not turn to the answer until you have completed all parts of the Assessment.

Practice devolved assessments

Chang Fashions Ltd

The tasks and questions are based on the transactions of Chang Fashions Ltd. The company owns a chain of clothes shops and has its head office located in premises in London. The head office has good storage facilities for stock held, substantial sales areas for both men's and ladies' wear and office space for the administrative staff employed within the company.

The Managing Director is Mary Chang and Rahul Divan is the Accountant and Company Secretary. You are employed as an Accounting Technician to assist Rahul Divan.

DATA

The following transactions all occurred during the week ended 2 December 20X4 and have been entered for you into summarised books of original entry. VAT has been calculated to the nearest pound at a rate of 17.5% and you should continue to use this rate for any subsequent calculations.

'Other customers' and 'other suppliers' should each be treated as individual accounts.

Purchases invoices received

	Total £	VAT £	Net £	Goods for resale £	Power and heating £
Style Clothes Ltd	9,736	1,450	8,286	8,286	
South East Electric	3,550	529	3,021		3,021
Southern Gas	3,108	463	2,645		2,645
Trend Imports Ltd	17,907	2,667	15,240	15,240	
Other suppliers	20,935	3,118	17,817	17,817	
	55,236	8,227	47,009	41,343	5,666

Purchases returns day book

	Total £	VAT £	Net £
Style Clothes Ltd	256	38	218

Cash book

				£	
Opening balance at start of week				28,619	(credit)

Receipts

		VAT	Total received	
		£	£	
Cash sales		7,770	52,170	
Bank interest			411	
				52,581
				23,962

Payments

	Discount	VAT	Total paid	
	£	£	£	
Cash purchases		205	1,376	
Style Clothes Ltd	160		7,420	
Southern Gas			1,204	
Shop fittings purchased		244	1,640	
Shop fittings repaired		13	88	
Refunds for returns		41	275	
Other suppliers			12,143	
				24,146
Closing balance at end of week				184 (credit)

The following balances are available to you at the start of the week ended 2 December 20X4.

Suppliers

	£
Style Clothes Ltd	32,417
South East Electric	NIL
Southern Gas	1,204
Trend Imports Ltd	45,862
Other suppliers	98,291

Other

Purchases	1,066,213
Sales	1,453,420
Purchases returns	5,741
Sales returns	6,984
Power and heating	7,122
Shop fittings	35,560
Shop fittings repairs	241
Bank interest received	319
VAT (credit balance)	38,162
Discount received	4,337
Creditors control account	177,774
Various other debit balances: total	1,542,632
Various other credit balances: total	950,380

Practice devolved assessments

COMPLETE ALL THE FOLLOWING TASKS.

Task 1 Enter the opening balances into the following accounts:
Creditors control account
Power and heating
Purchases
Sales returns
Shop fittings
VAT
Southern Gas
Style Clothes Ltd

These accounts can be found on pages 43 to 45.

Task 2 Enter all relevant entries into the accounts shown in Task 1.

Task 3 Balance off all the accounts in which you have made entries in Task 1.

Task 4 Calculate the closing balances of the remaining accounts. Complete the trial balance on page 46 by inserting the updated figure for each account in either the debit balances column or the credit balances column as appropriate. Total the two columns. The two totals should be the same. If they do not agree, try to trace and correct any errors you may have made within the time you have available. If you are still unable to make the totals balance, leave the work incomplete. (In checking for errors you should take into account that the total of the suppliers' balances should be the same figure as the balance of the creditors control account.)

Note It is not a requirement to draw up all the individual accounts in order to calculate the closing balances for Task 4. Candidates may, however, adopt that approach if they wish.

GENERAL LEDGER

Creditors Control Account

Date	Details	Amount £	Date	Details	Amount £

Power and Heating

Date	Details	Amount £	Date	Details	Amount £

Purchases

Date	Details	Amount £	Date	Details	Amount £

Practice devolved assessments

Sales Returns

Date	Details	Amount £	Date	Details	Amount £

Shop Fittings

Date	Details	Amount £	Date	Details	Amount £

VAT

Date	Details	Amount £	Date	Details	Amount £

CREDITORS LEDGER

Southern Gas

Date	Details	Amount £	Date	Details	Amount £

Style Clothes Limited

Date	Details	Amount £	Date	Details	Amount £

Practice devolved assessments

TRIAL BALANCE AT THE END OF THE WEEK

	Debit balances £	Credit balances £
Suppliers	....	....
Style Clothes Ltd	....	....
South East Electric	....	....
Southern Gas	....	....
Trend Imports Ltd	....	....
Other suppliers	....	....
Total of suppliers	....	....
Other		
Bank	....	....
Purchases	....	....
Sales	....	....
Purchases returns	....	....
Sales returns	....	....
Power and heating	....	....
Shop fittings	....	....
Shop fittings repairs	....	....
Bank interest received	....	....
VAT	....	....
Discount received	....	....
Other debit balances	1,542,632	
Other credit balances		950,380
Totals		

Practice devolved assessment
3 MEL Motor Factors

Performance criteria

The following performance criteria are covered in this Devolved Assessment.

Element 3.1 Balance bank transactions

1 Details from the relevant primary documentation are recorded in the cash book

2 Totals and balances of receipts and payments are correctly calculated

3 Individual items on the bank statement and in the cash book are compared for accuracy

Element 3.2 Prepare ledger balances and control accounts

1 Relevant accounts are totalled

3 Authorised adjustments are correctly processed and documented

Notes on completing the Assessment

This Assessment is designed to test your ability to post transactions correctly to the cash book, including items on the bank statement, and to post and total the ledgers.

You are allowed 2 hours to complete your work.

A high level of accuracy is required. Check your work carefully.

Correcting fluid may be used but should be used in moderation. Errors should be crossed out neatly and clearly. You should write in black ink and not in pencil.

A full answer to this Assessment is provided on page 185 of this Kit.

Do not turn to the answer until you have completed all parts of the Assessment.

Practice devolved assessments

MEL Motor Factors

The tasks and questions are all centred on the activities of MEL Motor Factors Ltd. The company trades in motor parts and accessories and is based in Manchester in the UK. Although customers are located entirely in the UK, goods supplied originate from both the UK and overseas.

The Managing Director is Andrew Bolton and Cathy Payne is the Accountant. You are employed as an Accounting Technician to assist Cathy Payne.

DATA

The following transactions all occurred on 1 June 20X5 and have yet to be entered into the ledger system. VAT has been calculated to the nearest pound at a rate of 17.5% and you should continue to use this rate for any subsequent calculations. The bank statement was received on 2 June but again contains transactions relating to 1 June.

(a) *Sales invoices issued*

	Total £	VAT £	Net £
Autoparts Ltd	5,492	818	4,674
Salfords Stores Ltd	3,396	506	2,890
Motormania	6,156	917	5,239
Other customers	22,696	3,380	19,316
	37,740	5,621	32,119

(b) *Purchase invoices received*

	Total £	VAT £	Net £
Carmart Imports Ltd	8,371	1,247	7,124
Lombard Products Ltd	7,727	1,151	6,576
Lucas & Co	5,820	867	4,953
Other suppliers	12,676	1,888	10,788
	34,594	5,153	29,441

(c) *Credit note issued*

	Total £	VAT £	Net £
Motormania	168	25	143

(d) *Journal entries*

	Debit £	Credit £
Creditors control account	1,450	
Debtors control account		1,450
Correction of an error made 10 May 20X5		

(e) *Cheques issued*

	£
Lombard Products Ltd	2,817
(In full repayment of a debt for £2,958)	
Cash purchases	1,363
(Inclusive of VAT of £203)	

(f) *Cheques received*

	£
Motormania	1,472
(In full repayment of a debt for £1,550)	

(g) *Bank statement received*

Royal Bank Ltd
MEL Motor Factors Ltd
Statement of Account

Account No: 40319442

Date	Details	Debit	Credit	Balance
		£	£	£
1 June	Balance forward			4,120
1 June	Bank interest		122	4,242
1 June	Bank charges	210		4,032

The following balances are available to you at the start of the day on 1 June 20X5.

Customers

	£
Autoparts Ltd	24,617
Salfords Stores Ltd	41,561
Motormania	27,124
Other customers	627,341

Suppliers

	£
Carmart Imports Ltd	28,413
Lombard Products Ltd	56,987
Lucas & Co	33,792
Other suppliers	492,853

Other

	£
Purchases	2,652,194
Sales	3,122,786
Sales returns	6,225
Bank (debit balance)	4,120
Bank charges	261
Bank interest received	103
VAT (credit balance)	71,089
Discount allowed	21,408
Discount received	15,194
Debtors control account	720,643
Creditors control account	612,045
Various other debit balances: total	1,431,500
Various other credit balances: total	1,015,134

Complete all the following tasks.

Practice devolved assessments

Task 1

Enter the opening balances into the following accounts.

> Bank (cash book)
> Bank charges
> Bank interest received
> Debtors control account
> Discount allowed
> Discount received
> Purchases
> VAT
> Lombard Products Ltd
> Motormania

These accounts can be found on pages 50 to 52.

Task 2

Using the data shown on pages 48 and 49, enter all relevant transactions into the accounts shown in Task 1. Please note that the cash book has been divided into two sections, one to record receipts and the other to record payments. When making entries in the cash book, ensure that you complete the analysis columns and that you include the two items shown in the bank statement on page 49.

Task 3

Total the various columns of the cash book and clearly show the closing bank balance.

Task 4

Transfer any relevant sums from the cash book into the other accounts shown in Task 1 to complete the necessary double entry for those accounts.

Task 5

Balance off all the remaining accounts in which you have made entries.

Note. You are not required to update any accounts other than those shown in Task 1.

General ledger

RECEIPTS: CASH BOOK

Date	Details	Discounts £	Total received £	VAT £	Debtors £	Other £

PAYMENTS: CASH BOOK

Date	Details	Discounts £	Total paid £	VAT £	Creditors £	Other £

BANK CHARGES

Date	Details	Amount £	Date	Details	Amount £

BANK INTEREST RECEIVED

Date	Details	Amount £	Date	Details	Amount £

DEBTORS CONTROL ACCOUNT

Date	Details	Amount £	Date	Details	Amount £

DISCOUNT ALLOWED

Date	Details	Amount £	Date	Details	Amount £

DISCOUNT RECEIVED

Date	Details	Amount £	Date	Details	Amount £

PURCHASES

Date	Details	Amount £	Date	Details	Amount £

VAT

Date	Details	Amount £	Date	Details	Amount £

Creditors ledger

LOMBARD PRODUCTS LTD

Date	Details	Amount £	Date	Details	Amount £

Debtors ledger

MOTORMANIA

Date	Details	Amount £	Date	Details	Amount £

4 Practice devolved assessment
Music World

Performance criteria

The following performance criteria are covered in this Devolved Assessment.

Element 3.2 Prepare ledger balances and control accounts

1 Relevant accounts are totalled

3 Authorised adjustments are correctly processed and documented

Element 3.3 Draft an initial trial balance

1 Information required for the initial trial balance is identified and obtained from the relevant sources

3 The draft initial trial balance is prepared in line with the organisation's policies and procedures

Notes on completing the Assessment

This Assessment is designed to test your ability to post transactions correctly to the ledgers and prepare an initial trial balance.

You are allowed 2 hours to complete your work.

A high level of accuracy is required. Check your work carefully.

Correcting fluid may be used but should be used in moderation. Errors should be crossed out neatly and clearly. You should write in black ink and not in pencil.

A full answer to this Assessment is provided on page 188 of this Kit.

Do not turn to the answer until you have completed all parts of the Assessment.

Practice devolved assessments

Music World

The tasks and questions are all based on the transactions of Music World Ltd. The company operates as a wholesaler supplying cassette tapes and compact discs throughout the UK.

The Managing Director is Jane Alder whilst Tony Bryant is the Accountant and Company Secretary. You are employed as an Accounting Technician to assist Tony Bryant.

DATA

The following transactions all occurred on 1 December 20X3 and have been entered for you into summarised books of original entry. VAT has been calculated to the nearest pound at a rate of 17.5% and you should continue to use this rate for any subsequent calculations.

Treat 'other customers' and 'other suppliers' as individual accounts.

SALES DAY BOOK

	Total £	VAT £	Net £
Hit Records Ltd	4,279	637	3,642
Smiths & Co	6,023	897	5,126
Classic Music	1,978	295	1,683
Other customers	12,307	1,833	10,474
	24,587	3,662	20,925

PURCHASES DAY BOOK

	Total £	VAT £	Net £	Goods for resale £	Heating & lighting £
HMI Ltd	10,524	1,567	8,957	8,957	
Atlantic Imports Ltd	12,528	1,866	10,662	10,662	
Southern Electric	606	90	516		516
Other suppliers	5,652	842	4,810	4,810	
	29,310	4,365	24,945	24,429	516

SALES RETURNS DAY BOOK

	Total £	VAT £	Net £
Classic Music	167	25	142

PURCHASES RETURNS DAY BOOK

	Total £	VAT £	Net £
Atlantic Imports Ltd	32	5	27

Practice devolved assessments

CASH BOOK

			£	
Opening balance at start of day			14,492	(debit)

Receipts	Discount £	Amount received £		
Classic Music	45	1,755		
			1,755	
			16,247	

Payments	Discount £	Total amount paid £	VAT £	
Atlantic Imports Ltd	112	4,388		
Equipment purchased		970	144	
Equipment repairs		102	15	
Unpaid cheque - Classic Music		1,000		
Bank charges		67		
Cash purchases		230	34	
Other suppliers		10,565		
			17,322	
Closing balance at end of day			1,075	(credit)

The following balances are available to you at the start of the day on 1 December 20X3.

	£
Customers	
Hit records Ltd	10,841
Smiths & Co Ltd	18,198
Classic Music	16,742
Other customers	491,702
Suppliers	
HMI Ltd	82,719
Atlantic Imports Ltd	43,607
Southern Electric	nil
Other suppliers	278,220
Other	
Purchases	2,432,679
Sales	3,284,782
Sales returns	10,973
Purchases returns	9,817
Heating and lighting	1,728
Equipment	4,182
Equipment repairs	166
Bank charges	82
VAT (credit balance)	63,217
Discount allowed	11,420
Discount received	8,516
Debtors control account	537,483
Creditors control account	404,546
Various other debit balances (total)	1,368,815
Various other credit balances (total)	611,142

Task 1

Enter the opening balances into the following accounts.

(a) Debtors control account
(b) Creditors control account
(c) Equipment
(d) Heating and lighting

Practice devolved assessments

(e) Purchases
(f) VAT
(g) Classic Music
(h) Atlantic Imports Ltd.

These accounts can be found on pages 56 to 58.

Task 2

Enter all relevant entries into the accounts shown in Task 1.

Task 3

Balance off all the accounts in which you have made entries in Task 2.

Task 4

Calculate the closing balances of the remaining accounts. Complete the trial balance on page 59 by inserting the updated figure for each account in either the debit balances column or the credit balances column as appropriate. Total the two columns. The two totals should be the same. If they do not agree try to trace and correct any errors you have made within the time you have available. If you are still unable to make the totals balance, leave the work incomplete.

Note. It is not a requirement to draw up all the individual accounts in order to calculate the closing balances for Task 4. Candidates may, however, adopt that approach if they wish.

General ledger

DEBTORS CONTROL ACCOUNT

Date	Details	Amount £	Date	Details	Amount £

CREDITORS CONTROL ACCOUNT

Date	Details	Amount £	Date	Details	Amount £

EQUIPMENT

Date	Details	Amount £	Date	Details	Amount £

HEATING & LIGHTING

Date	Details	Amount £	Date	Details	Amount £

PURCHASES

Date	Details	Amount £	Date	Details	Amount £

VAT

Date	Details	Amount £	Date	Details	Amount £

Practice devolved assessments

Debtors ledger

CLASSIC MUSIC

Date	Details	Amount £	Date	Details	Amount £

Creditors ledger

ATLANTIC IMPORTS LTD

Date	Details	Amount £	Date	Details	Amount £

Practice devolved assessments

Updated trial balance at the end of the day

	Debit balances £	Credit balances £
Customers		
Hit Records Ltd	....	....
Smiths & Co	....	....
Classic Music	....	....
Other customers	....	....
Suppliers		
HMI Ltd	....	....
Atlantic Imports Ltd	....	....
Southern Electric	....	....
Other suppliers	....	....
Purchases	....	....
Sales	....	....
Sales returns	....	....
Purchases returns	....	....
Heating & lighting	....	....
Equipment	....	....
Equipment repairs	....	....
Bank charges	....	....
VAT	....	....
Bank	....	....
Discount allowed	....	....
Discount received	....	....
Other debit balances	1,368,815	....
Other credit balances		611,142
Totals		

Trial run devolved assessments

TRIAL RUN DEVOLVED ASSESSMENT
T S STATIONERY

FOUNDATION STAGE - NVQ/SVQ2

Unit 3

Preparing Ledger Balances and an Initial Trial Balance

The purpose of this Trial Run Devolved Assessment is to give you an idea of what an AAT simulation looks like. It is not intended as a definitive guide to the tasks you may be required to perform.

The suggested time allowance for this Assessment is **three hours**. Up to 30 minutes extra time may be permitted in an AAT simulation. Breaks in assessment will be allowed in the AAT simulation, but it must normally be completed in one day.

Calculators may be used but no reference material is permitted.

**DO NOT OPEN THIS PAPER UNTIL YOU ARE READY TO START
UNDER TIMED CONDITIONS**

Trial run devolved assessment

INSTRUCTIONS

This Assessment is designed to test your ability to prepare ledger cash balances and an initial trial balance.

The situation is provided on Page 65.

The tasks you are to perform are set out within the data.

You are allowed three hours to complete your work.

A high level of accuracy is required. Check your work carefully.

Correcting fluid may be used but should be used in moderation. Errors should be crossed out neatly and clearly. You should write in black ink, not pencil.

You are advised to read the whole of the Assessment before commencing as all of the information may be of value and is not necessarily supplied in the sequence in which you might wish to deal with it.

A full suggested answer to this Assessment is provided on Page 193 of this Kit.

Trial run devolved assessment

INTRODUCTION

- You are the bookkeeper for a small business supplying decorative and unusual stationery and cards called T S Stationery.

- The accounting system is a manual system with all double entry taking place in the main ledger and subsidiary ledgers kept for debtors and creditors.

- Today is 2 April 20X1 and you are trying to prepare the trial balance for the year ended 31 March 20X1.

- Before preparing the trial balance there are a number of accounting tasks for the last few days of March that must be undertaken.

Task 1

The purchases day book and purchases returns day book has not yet been posted for the last week in March. The two day books are given below together with the relevant main ledger accounts and subsidiary ledger accounts. You are required to update the ledger accounts to reflect the entries in the day books.

PURCHASES DAY BOOK

Supplier	*Gross* £	*VAT* £	*Net* £
FP Paper	188	28	160
Gift Products Ltd	235	35	200
Harper Bros	141	21	120
J S Traders	282	42	240
	846	126	720

PURCHASES RETURNS DAY BOOK

Supplier	*Gross* £	*VAT* £	*Net* £
Gift Products Ltd	94	14	80
Harper Bros	47	7	40
	141	21	120

Trial run devolved assessment

MAIN LEDGER ACCOUNTS

CREDITORS CONTROL ACCOUNT

	£			£
		27 Mar	Opening balance	14,325

PURCHASES ACCOUNT

		£		£
27 Mar	Opening balance	166,280		

PURCHASES RETURNS ACCOUNT

	£			£
		27 Mar	Opening balance	4,180

VAT ACCOUNT

	£			£
		27 Mar	Opening balance	1,405

SUBSIDIARY LEDGER ACCOUNTS

F P PAPER

	£			£
		27 Mar	Opening balance	3,825

GIFT PRODUCTS LIMITED

	£			£
		27 Mar	Opening balance	4,661

HARPER BROS

	£			£
		27 Mar	Opening balance	3,702

J S TRADERS

	£			£
		27 Mar	Opening balance	2,137

Trial run devolved assessment

Task 2

Reconcile the balance on the creditors control account with the total of the four creditor balances (these are the only credit suppliers of the business).

You are to now balance the purchases account, purchases returns account and VAT account.

Task 3

Journal number 336

	£	£
Bad debtors expense	400	
Debtors control		400

Being write off of bad debt from C Cummings

Journal number 337

	£	£
Debtors control	100	
Sales		100

Being undercast of sales day book

The relevant main ledger accounts are given below. You are also given all of the individual debtor accounts from the subsidiary ledger.

Enter the journal entries in the relevant main ledger and subsidiary ledger accounts and then reconcile the balance on the debtors control account to the total of the individual debtor accounts in the subsidiary ledger.

You can now balance the sales account and the bad debts expense account.

MAIN LEDGER

DEBTORS CONTROL ACCOUNT

		£		£
31 Mar	Balance b/d	23,230		

SALES ACCOUNT

	£			£
		31 Mar	Balance b/d	255,810

BAD DEBTS EXPENSE ACCOUNT

£	£

SUBSIDIARY LEDGER

RETAIL ENTERPRISES

		£		£
31 Mar	Balance b/d	5,114		

C CUMMINGS

		£		£
31 Mar	Balance b/d	400		

PALMER LIMITED

	£		£
31 Mar Balance b/d	6,248		

REAPERS STORES

	£		£
31 Mar Balance b/d	5,993		

KNIGHT RETAIL

	£		£
31 Mar Balance b/d	5,575		

Task 4

Given below is the cash receipts and payments book for the business for the month of March 20X1. You are also given the bank statement for the month.

You are required to check the cash book carefully to the bank statement and adjust the cash book for any missing entries.

CASH BOOK

RECEIPTS			PAYMENTS			
Date	Detail	£	Date	Detail	Cheque no	£
1 Mar	Balance b/d	3,668	5 Mar	Harper Bros	002643	2,558
7 Mar	Palmer Ltd	2,557	12 Mar	Gift Products	002644	3,119
15 Mar	Retail Engineering	4,110	18 Mar	F P Paper	002645	2,553
20 Mar	Reapers Stores	4,782	24 Mar	J S Traders	002646	983
28 Mar	Knight Retail	3,765	31 Mar	BACS – wages		3,405

NORTHERN BANK
Royal Bank House
Trestle Square
Sandefield
SF2 3HS

Cheque account: T S Stationery   Account number 10364382

SHEET 0124

		Paid out £	Paid in £	Balance £
1 Mar	Balance b/d			3,668
10 Mar	Credit		2,557	6,225
16 Mar	Cheque 002644	3,119		3,106
20 Mar	Credit		4,110	7,216
22 Mar	Cheque 002643	2,558		
	SO - District Council: rates	200		4,458
25 Mar	Credit		4,782	9,240
26 Mar	Cheque 002645	2,553		
	SO - Loan repayment	400		6,287
30 Mar	Interest		20	6,307
31 Mar	BACS	3,405		2,902

Task 5

Total and balance the adjusted cash book and complete the double entry in the ledger accounts given. You can then balance each of the ledger accounts.

Trial run devolved assessment

RATES ACCOUNT

		£			£
31 Mar	Balance b/d	2,200			

LOAN ACCOUNT

		£			£
			31 Mar	Balance b/d	6,400

BANK INTEREST RECEIVABLE

		£			£
			31 Mar	Balance b/d	100

Task 6

Make a note of the reasons why the cash book balance is not equal to the bank statement balance.

Task 7

T S Stationery has three monthly paid employees, including yourself. The wages book for March is given below. The details have not yet been entered into the ledger accounts, although the payment of the net pay has been entered in the cash payments book. You are required to enter the totals in the relevant ledger accounts given and to balance the accounts.

	Gross Pay £	PAYE £	Employee's NIC £	Employer's NIC £	Net Pay £
M Savage	2,000	350	175	200	1,475
T Stiles	1,500	240	125	140	1,135
L Fraser	1,000	130	75	80	795
	4,500	720	375	420	3,405

WAGES CONTROL ACCOUNT

£	£

WAGES EXPENSE ACCOUNT

£	£
1 Mar Balance b/d 54,120	

INLAND REVENUE ACCOUNT

£	£

Trial run devolved assessment

Task 8

The petty cash is run on an imprest system of £100 per month.

The petty cash vouchers in the petty cash box at 31 March were:

Voucher number	£
0264	3.67
0265	9.48
0266	6.70
0267	13.20
0268	2.36
0269	1.55
0270	10.46
0271	4.89
0272	3.69

The cash in the petty cash box was:

Note/coin	Number
£10	1
£5	4
£2	2
£1	7
50p	3
20p	4
10p	5
5p	1
2p	7
1p	1

Reconcile the petty cash vouchers and the petty cash and determine the amount that will appear in the trial balance for petty cash.

Task 9

Given below are two stores records cards for two of T S Stationery's products, product code X2635 and F3398.

Stores record - Product code X2635

		Quantity in	Quantity out	Balance
1 March	Opening balance			120
7 March		200		320
10 March			80	240
15 March			105	135
17 March			90	45
20 March		200		245
28 March			120	125

Stores record - Product code F3398

		Quantity in	Quantity out	Balance
1 March	Opening balance			40
2 March		150		190
8 March			155	35
12 March		150		185
20 March			150	35
22 March		150		185
27 March			160	25

The physical stock count at 31 March 20X1 revealed that there were 120 units of product X2635 in stock and 175 units of F3398.

Suggest reasons why the physical amount of stock for each of these products does not agree with the stores records.

Task 10

You are now ready to prepare the initial balance at the year end, 31 March 20X1. Given below are the ledger balances at 31 March 20X1 which must be completed with the balances from the ledger accounts dealt with in earlier tasks.

You are required to prepare the initial trial balance at 31 March 20X1.

	£
Building	100,000
Motor vehicles	34,500
Office equipment	13,000
Purchases	Own figure
Purchases returns	Own figure
Capital	160,000
Sales	Own figure
Sales returns	6,800
Discounts allowed	300
Stock	16,000
Loan	Own figure
Discount received	600
Debtors	Own figure
Petty cash	Own figure
Creditors	Own figure
VAT	Own figure
Bank	Own figure
Inland revenue	Own figure
Wages	Own figure
Motor expenses	4,297
Telephone	4,850
Electricity	3,630
Rates	Own figure
Miscellaneous expenses	2,900
Bad debts expense	Own figure
Bank interest receivable	Own figure

Task 11

The owner of the business is delighted that the initial trial balance does in fact balance and has said to you that he therefore assumes this means that all of the accounting entries are correct.

You are required to write a memo to the owner explaining what types of errors there may be in the accounting records that are not shown up by the trial balance using examples of how these errors could take place in T S Stationery's books but still not cause an imbalance on the trial balance.

COVERAGE OF PERFORMANCE CRITERA

All performance criteria in Unit 3 are covered by this trial run devolved assessment.

Element	PC coverage
3.1	**Balance bank transactions**
	Details from the relevant primary documentation are recorded in the cash book.
	Totals and balances of receipts and payments are correctly calculated.
	Individual items on the bank statement and in the cash book are compared for accuracy.
	Discrepancies are identified and referred to the appropriate person.
3.2	**Prepare ledger balances and control accounts**
	Relevant accounts are totalled.
	control accounts are reconciled with the total of the balance in the subsidiary ledger, where appropriate.
	Authorised adjustments are correctly processed and documented.
	Discrepancies arising from the reconciliation of control accounts are either resolved or referred to the appropriate person.
	Documentation is stored securely and in line with the organisation's confidentiality requirements.
3.3	**Draft an initial trial balance**
	Information required for the initial trial balance is identified and obtained from the relevant sources.
	Relevant people are asked for advice when the necessary information is not available.
	The draft initial trial balance is prepared in line with the organisation's policies and procedures.
	Discrepancies are identified in the balancing process and referred to the appropriate person.

Range

The following range statements will need to be assessed by other means, eg work documents, written activities.

3.1 Discrepancies: uncertainty in coding

3.3 Discrepancies: incorrect double entries and wrong calculations (although both of these may occur naturally throughout performance in the assessment)

Knowledge and understanding

Whilst some areas of knowledge and understanding can be inferred through performance, there will be gaps in evidence which should be plugged by other assessment methods, eg questioning.

Centres are reminded that there should be a mix of evidence across the unit, simulations cannot stand alone as evidence of competent performance, and the evidence in the portfolio should be mapped clearly to the student record.

AAT SAMPLE SIMULATION

FOUNDATION STAGE - NVQ/SVQ2

Unit 3

Preparing Ledger Balances and an Initial Trial Balance

The suggested time allowance for this Assessment is three hours, 1½ hours for Part 1 and 1½ hours for Part 2. Up to 30 minutes extra time may be permitted in an AAT simulation. Breaks in assessment will be allowed in the AAT simulation, but it must normally be completed in one day.

Calculators may be used but no reference material is permitted.

**DO NOT OPEN THIS PAPER UNTIL YOU ARE READY TO START
UNDER TIMED CONDITIONS**

AAT sample simulation

INSTRUCTIONS

This simulation is designed to test your ability to prepare ledger balances and an initial trial balance.

The situation is provided on Page 81

The simulation is divided into two parts, as follows.

Part one: prepare balances

Task 1 Prepare account and reconcile balances
Task 2 Adjust and total accounts
Task 3 Reconcile balance, identify errors
Task 4 Prepare a trial balance and report any imbalance
Task 5 Suggest improvements to security

Part two: prepare and reconcile accounts

Task 6   Update cash book
Task 7   Check bank statement
Task 8   Total cash book
Task 9   Explain imbalance
Task 10 Complete double entry
Task 11 Prepare and total wages control account
Task 12 Complete stores record, reconcile with stock check
Task 13 Complete trial balance

The simulation can be attempted either in one sitting of **three hours** or in two sittings (one for each part) of **one hour and 30 minutes** each, separated by not more than one week. Your AAC will have told you which way you are doing the simulation.

If you are doing the simulation in one sitting, you should read all the information on pages 81 to 96 before starting.

If you are doing the simulation in two sittings, you should read:

- Up to page 88 before starting Part 1
- Pages 89 to 96 before starting Part 2

Your answers should be set out in this booklet, in the spaces indicated and using the forms provided. If you require additional answer pages, ask the person in charge.

A high level of accuracy is required. Check your work carefully before handing it in.

Correcting fluid may be used but only in moderation. Any errors should be crossed out neatly and clearly. The use of pencils for your written answers is not acceptable.

You are reminded that you should not bring any unauthorised material, such as books or notes, in the simulation. If you have any such material you should surrender it to the assessor immediately.

Any instances of misconduct will be brought to the attention of the AAT, and disciplinary action may be taken.

A full suggested answer to this simulation is provided on page 203 of the kit.

SITUATION

Wentworth Cleaners is an organisation that buys and sells industrial vacuum cleaners.

The workforce consists of the accountant and manager (Carolyn Allday), a driver (Jennifer Stone) and warehouseman (Barry Glazier) and you, the bookkeeper.

The business operates a manual accounting system but the monthly salaries are completed using a computerised system. You are the bookkeeper but have only recently commenced your duties, After some time spent with Carolyn familiarising you with the organisation, its policies and procedures, you are now ready to start work on the accounting records.

Assume today's date is 4 October 20X0.

PART 1

THE TASKS TO BE PERFORMED

Following the departure of the last bookkeeper some end of month tasks for August remained outstanding.

Task 1   A list of subsidiary (purchases) ledger balances is shown on Page 83 together with a summary of activity in the month. Prepare a creditors control account as at 31 August 20X0, showing clearly the balance carried down, and reconcile this balance with the list of balances in the subsidiary (purchases) ledger. Assume all the relevant double entries have been made. Record your answer on Page 83.

Task 2   The journal entry file contains approved journal entries, shown on Page 84, which have not yet been processed. Using this journal entry sheet, adjust the relevant accounts on Pages 84 and 85. Total three of the accounts, bad debts written off, VAT and sales, and show clearly the balances carried down.

Task 3   Using the summary of activity shown on Page 85, complete the debtors control account, showing clearly the balance carried down. Use the list of balances in the subsidiary (sales) ledger to reconcile this balance with the debtors control account. If there is an imbalance make a note to Carolyn, suggesting where the error may be. Record your answer on Pages 85 and 86.

Task 4   Using the list of balances Carolyn has provided you with, on Page 86 and the balances you have calculated, prepare a trial balance for month ended 31 August 20X0, using the form on Page 87. If you find there is an imbalance, make a note for Carloyn on the top half of Page 88.

Task 5   Carolyn has emphasised the need to keep all accounting information confidential. However, the ledgers have always been kept on the top of your desk, which is in reception. Make a further note to Carolyn on Page 88 suggesting any improvements you may consider appropriate.

DATA

Details for reconciliation of the creditors control account

Summary of activity

	£
Opening balance at 1 August 20X0	33,600
Purchases in August	31,725
Purchases returns in August	940
Discounts received	100
Bank payments to creditors	34,155

CREDITORS CONTROL ACCOUNT

Date	Details	Amount £	Date	Details	Amount £

Balances in subsidiary (purchases) ledger

JBS Controls	9,635
LTP Ltd	7,050
Edwards & Byng	5,875
J J Patel	4,700
KKB Ltd	2,870

RECONCILIATION OF CREDITORS CONTROL ACCOUNT
WITH SUBSIDIARY (PURCHASES) LEDGER
AT 31 AUGUST 20X0

	£
Closing balance of creditors control account	
Total balance of accounts in subsidiary (purchases) ledger	_____
Imbalance	_____

AAT sample simulation

THE JOURNAL

Reference	Date 20X0	Details	Dr £	Dr £
JNL 30	31 August	Bad debts written off VAT Debtors control account *To write off bad debts owned by JJ Hall – please note entries have already been made in subsidiary (sales) ledger*	600.00 105.00	 705.00
JNL 31	31 August	Sales Debtors control account *To adjust an error in posting to the sales account* **Approved:** *Carolyn Allday* **Date:** 30.08.X0	1.00	 1.00

BAD DEBTS WRITTEN OFF

Date 20X0	Details	Amount £	Date 20X0	Details	Amount £
31 August	Balance b/f	150			

VAT

Date 20X0	Details	Amount £	Date 20X0	Details	Amount £
31 August	Purchases	4,725	1 August	Balance b/f	14,269
31 August	Sales creditors	70	31 August	Purchase credits	140
			31 August	Sales	6,125

SALES

Date 20X0	Details	Amount £	Date 20X0	Details	Amount £
			1 August	Balance b/f	91,676
			31 August	Debtors	41,125

DEBTORS CONTROL ACCOUNT

Date 20X0	Details	Amount £	Date 20X0	Details	Amount £

Details for reconciliation of the debtors control account

Summary of activity

	£
Opening balance at 1 August 20X0	91,403
Sales in August	41,125
Sales returns in August	470
Discounts allowed	50
Bank receipts from debtors	36,824

Balances in subsidiary (sales) ledger

	£
J Owen Ltd	14,571
B Flynn & Company	8,000
Keeley & Company	19,200
Instone Industries	23,018
Cosmic Cleaners	15,017
Leasowes Ltd (credit balance)	(224)
Roberts & Company	14,448

RECONCILIATION OF DEBTORS CONTROL ACCOUNT WITH SUBIDIARY (SALES) LEDGER AT 31 AUGUST 20X0

	£
Closing balance of debtors control account	
Total balance of accounts in subsidiary (sales) ledger	_____
Imbalance	

NOTE TO CAROLYN

LIST OF BALANCES AS AT 31 AUGUST 20X0

	£
Motor vehicle	21,500
Office equipment	2,000
Stock	34,800
Bank (debit balance)	6,700
Debtors control	Own figure
Creditors control	Own figure
VAT	Own figure
Capital	99,200
Loan from bank	2,200
Sales	Own figure
Sales returns	1,175
Purchases	94,876
Purchases returns	200
Bank charges	50
Discounts allowed	60
Discounts received	160
Wages	18,346
Rent and rates	1,080
Electricity	800
Telephone	756
Motor expenses	2,470
Bad debts written off	Own figure

AAT sample simulation

TRIAL BALANCE AS AT 31 AUGUST 20X0

	Debit £	Credit £
Motor vehicle	_____	_____
Office equipment	_____	_____
Stock	_____	_____
Bank	_____	_____
Debtors control	_____	_____
Creditors control	_____	_____
VAT	_____	_____
Capital	_____	_____
Loan from bank	_____	_____
Sales	_____	_____
Sales returns	_____	_____
Purchases	_____	_____
Purchases returns	_____	_____
Bank charges	_____	_____
Discounts allowed	_____	_____
Discounts received	_____	_____
Wages	_____	_____
Rent and rates	_____	_____
Electricity	_____	_____
Telephone	_____	_____
Motor expenses	_____	_____
Bad debts written off	_____	_____
Miscellaneous expenses	_____	_____
Total	=======	=======

Note for Carolyn, Task 4

Note for Carolyn, Task 5

PART 2

THE TASKS TO BE PERFORMED

You are now able to begin preparing the accounts for month ended 30 September 20X0.

Task 6   Update the cash book on Page 91 from the standing order schedule and credit transfer schedule shown on Page 90.

Task 7   Check the bank statement on Page 90 against the cash book for accuracy, and update the cash book as necessary.

Task 8   Total the cash book, showing clearly the balance carried down.

Task 9   Using the paper provided on Page 91 list the reasons why the balance in the cash book does not agree with the balance on the bank statement.

Task 10   Complete the double entry in the main (nominal) ledger for any items you have added to the cash book using the accounts shown on Page 92 (assume entries to the subsidiary ledgers have been made). Total each account on Pages 92 and 93 showing clearly the balance carried down.

Carolyn has reconciled the debtors and creditors control accounts for September, you are to reconcile the wages control account and the stock control account.

Task 11   A summary of the salaries paid for the month of September is shown on Page 93. Entries have been made to the relevant main (general) ledger accounts and you are to prepare and total the wages control account, shown on Page 94.

Task 12   A physical stock check has been carried out on vacuum cleaner V800, which revealed a stock level of 139 items valued at £6,950. Referring to the details on Page 94 complete the stores record card and reconcile with the stock check figure. If there is an imbalance make a note to Carolyn pointing out where you think the difference may have occurred.

Task 13   Using the balance carried down when you totalled the cash book on Page 91, the balances you have calculated in the main (general) ledger on Pages 92 and 93, and list of balances given to you by Carolyn and shown on Page 95, complete the trial balance as at 30 September 20X0, shown on Page 96.

STANDING ORDER SCHEDULE

Due date	Details	£	Authorised by
15th of month April 20X0 to February 20X1 inclusive	East Council - Rates	150.00	*Carolyn Allday*
26th of month August 19X8 to July 20X1 inclusive	District Bank – Loan	200.00	*Carolyn Allday*
28th of month October 20X0 to September 20X1 inclusive	Bakers Rentals – Lease of van	250.00	*Carolyn Allday*

CREDIT TRANSFER SCHEDULE

Due date	Details	£	Authorised by
8th of month from January 20X0 until further notice	Centra Sales – Debtor	2,000.00	*Carolyn Allday*
15th of month from February 20X0 until further notice	Bradford Ltd – Debtor	1,000.00	*Carolyn Allday*

EAST BANK PLC
118 High Street, Northampton NT9 4BQ

To: Wentworth Cleaners   Account No 48104039   30 September 20X0

STATEMENT OF ACCOUNT

DATE 20X0	DETAILS	PAYMENTS £	RECEIPTS £	BALANCE £
1 Sept	Balance b/f			6,700
4 Sept	Cheque no 108300	600		6,100
1 Sept	Counter credit		200	6,300
8 Sept	Credit transfer: Centra Sales		2,000	8,300
10 Sept	Cheque No 108301	235		8,065
16 Sept	Standing order: East Council	150		7,915
24 Sept	Bank charges	66		7,849
25 Sept	Standing order: District Bank	200		7,649
30 Sept	Cheque No 108303	80		7,569
30 Sept	Credit transfer: Bradford Ltd		1,000	8,569
30 Sept	Salaries	4,512		4,057

CASH BOOK

Date 20X0	Details	Bank £	Date 20X0	Cheque number	Details	Bank £
1 Sept	Balance b/f	6,700	1 Sept	108300	J Green	600
1 Sept	L Townley	200	5 Sept	108301	Design Duo	235
28 Sept	Weston Wigg	1,200	25 Sept	108302	Carey Insurers	315
29 Sept	KKG Ltd	72	29 Sept	108303	Baxters Ltd	80
					Salaries	4,512

REASONS WHY THE CASH BOOK BALANCE DIFFERS FROM BANK STATEMENT

1 ....

....

2 ....

....

3 ....

....

AAT sample simulation

MAIN (NOMINAL) LEDGER

DEBTORS CONTROL ACCOUNT

Date 20X0	Details	Amount £	Date 20X0	Details	Amount £
1 Sept	Balance b/f	94,478	1 Sept	L Townley	200
30 Sept	Sales	47,000	28 Sept	Weston Wigg	1,200
			29 Sept	KKG Ltd	72

RENT AND RATES

Date 20X0	Details	Amount £	Date 20X0	Details	Amount £
1 Sept	Balance b/f	1,080			

LOAN

Date 20X0	Details	Amount £	Date 20X0	Details	Amount £
			1 Sept	Balance b/f	2,200

BANK CHARGES

Date 20X0	Details	Amount £	Date 20X0	Details	Amount £
1 Sept	Balance b/f	50			

PURCHASES

Date 20X0	Details	Amount £	Date 20X0	Details	Amount £
1 Sept	Balance b/f	94,876			
30 Sept	Creditors	9,774			

VAT

Date 20X0	Details	Amount £	Date 20X0	Details	Amount £
30 Sept	Purchases	1,710	1 Sept	Balance b/f	15,634
			30 Sept	Sales	7,000

CREDITORS CONTROL

Date 20X0	Details	Amount £	Date 20X0	Details	Amount £
1 Sept	J Green	600	1 Sept	Balance b/f	30,130
5 Sept	Design Duo	235	30 Sept	Purchases	11,484
25 Sept	Carey Insurers	315			
29 Sept	Baxters Ltd	80			

COMPUTER SUMMARY
SALARIES FOR MONTH ENDED 20.09.X0

Employee	Gross pay £	Tax £	Employees' NIC £	Employer's NIC £	Net pay £
Carolyn Allday	2,000.00	389.00	167.00	199.00	1,444.00
Jennifer Stone	1,690.00	290.00	140.00	160.00	1,260.00
Barry Glazier	1,140.00	145.00	85.00	95.00	910.00
A Student	1,100.00	125.00	77.00	89.00	898.00
	5,930.00	949.00	469.00	543.00	4,512.00

AAT sample simulation

WAGES CONTROL

Date 20X0	Details	Amount £	Date 20X0	Details	Amount £

STORES RECORD CARD – V800 INDUSTRIAL VACUUM CLEANER

Date	Details	In	Out	Quantity in stock	@ £50 per vacuum £
1 Sept	Opening balance			174	8,700
1 Sept	Sales		10	164	8,200
4 Sept	Sales		20	144	7,200
6 Sept	Sales		50	94	4,700
7 Sept	Sales		15		
11 Sept	Sales		20		
12 Sept	Faulty		1		
13 Sept	Sales		20		
15 Sept	Sales		20		
18 Sept	Receipt	100			
20 Sept	Sales		10		
22 Sept	Sales		5		
25 Sept	Sales		15		
26 Sept	Sales		20		
28 Sept	Receipt	110			
29 Sept	Sales		20		
30 Sept	Sales		20		

RECONCILIATION OF STOCK RECORD WITH PHYSICAL STOCK CHECK ON 30 SEPTEMBER 20X0

PHYSICAL STOCK CHECK 139 @ £50 ....

STORES RECORD CARD BALANCE ....

DIFFERENCE ....

Note for Carolyn

LIST OF BALANCES AS AT 30 SEPTEMBER 20X0

	£
Motor vehicle	21,500
Office equipment	2,000
Stock	34,800
Bank	Own figure
Debtors control	Own figure
Creditors control	Own figure
Inland Revenue	1,961
VAT	Own figure
Capital	99,200
Loan from bank	Own figure
Sales	172,800
Sales returns	1,175
Purchases	Own figure
Purchases returns	200
Bank charges	Own figure
Discounts allowed	60
Discounts received	160
Wages	24,819
Rent and rates	Own figure
Electricity	800
Telephone	756
Motor expenses	2,470
Bad debts written off	750
Miscellaneous expenses	483

AAT sample simulation

TRIAL BALANCE AS AT 30 SEPTEMBER 20X0

	Debit £	Credit £
Motor vehicle		
Office equipment		
Stock		
Bank		
Debtors control		
Creditors control		
Inland Revenue		
VAT		
Capital		
Loan from bank		
Sales		
Sales returns		
Purchases		
Purchases returns		
Bank charges		
Discounts allowed		
Discounts received		
Wages		
Rent and rates		
Electricity		
Telephone		
Motor expenses		
Bad debts written off		
Miscellaneous expenses		
Total		

AAT sample simulation

COVERAGE OF PERFORMANCE CRITERA

All performance criteria in Unit 3 are covered by this simulation.

Element	PC coverage
3.1	**Balance bank transactions**
	Details from the relevant primary documentation are recorded in the cash book.
	Totals and balances of receipts and payments are correctly calculated.
	Individual items on the bank statement and in the cash book are compared for accuracy.
	Discrepancies are identified and referred to the appropriate person.
3.2	**Prepare ledger balances and control accounts**
	Relevant accounts are totalled.
	control accounts are reconciled with the total of the balance in the subsidiary ledger, where appropriate.
	Authorised adjustments are correctly processed and documented.
	Discrepancies arising from the reconciliation of control accounts are either resolved or referred to the appropriate person.
	Documentation is stored securely and in line with the organisation's confidentiality requirements.
3.3	**Draft an initial trial balance**
	Information required for the initial trial balance is identified and obtained from the relevant sources.
	Relevant people are asked for advice when the necessary information is not available.
	The draft initial trial balance is prepared in line with the organisation's policies and procedures.
	Discrepancies are identified in the balancing process and referred to the appropriate person.

Range

The following range statements will need to be assessed by other means, eg work documents, written activities.

3.1 Discrepancies: uncertainty in coding

3.3 Discrepancies: incorrect double entries and wrong calculations (although both of these may occur naturally throughout performance in the simulation)

AAT sample simulation

Knowledge and understanding

Whilst some areas of knowledge and understanding can be inferred through performance, there will be gaps in evidence which should be plugged by other assessment methods, eg questioning.

Centres are reminded that there should be a mix of evidence across the unit, simulations cannot stand alone as evidence of competent performance, and the evidence in the portfolio should be mapped clearly to the student record.

Trial run central assessments

TRIAL RUN CENTRAL ASSESSMENT 1

FOUNDATION STAGE
REVISED STANDARDS
NVQ/SVQ LEVEL 2 IN ACCOUNTING

Preparing Ledger Balances
and an Initial Trial Balance

The Central Assessment is in two parts.

Section 1   Processing Exercise
             Complete all 5 tasks

Section 2   Ten Tasks and Questions
             Complete all tasks and questions

DO NOT OPEN THIS PAPER UNTIL YOU ARE READY TO START
UNDER TIMED CONDITIONS

Trial run central assessments

You are reminded that competence must be achieved in each section. You should therefore attempt and aim to complete EVERY task in BOTH sections. All essential workings should be included within your answers where appropriate

You are advised to spend 90 minutes on Section 1 and 90 minutes on Section 2.

INTRODUCTION

- JLW Ltd is a business manufacturing gold jewellery.
- The company supplies wholesale and retail customers.
- The company sells its products in its own retail shops.
- The company's Accountant is Carol Chang.
- You are an Accounting Technician employed to assist Carol Chang.

DATA

Transactions

The transactions, which occurred on 1 June 20X7, have been recorded in the sales day book, the sales returns day book and the cash book (given below) but have not yet been entered into the ledger system. VAT has been calculated at a rate of 17.5%.

SALES DAY BOOK

Date	Details	Invoice no	Net	VAT	Gross
20X7			£	£	£
1 June	H Stanton plc	DB/21807	5,760	1,008	6,768
1 June	J Llewellyn & Sons Ltd	DB/21808	1,600	280	1,880
1 June	York Jewellers	DB/21809	2,240	392	2,632
1 June	H Stanton plc	DB/21810	6,400	1,120	7,520
1 June	Bijoux Ltd	DB/21811	1,440	252	1,692
1 June	York Jewellers	DB/21812	800	140	940
Totals			18,240	3,192	21,432

SALES RETURNS DAY BOOK

Date	Details	Credit note no	Net	VAT	Gross
20X7			£	£	£
1 June	H Stanton plc	CR2276	320	56	376
1 June	J Llewellyn & Sons Ltd	CR2277	400	70	470
Totals			720	126	846

CASH BOOK

Date	Details	Discount allowed	Cash	Bank	Date	Details	Discount received	Cash	Bank
20X7		£	£	£			£	£	£
1 June	Balances b/d		80	6,860	1 June	Gee & Law			100
1 June	Bijoux Ltd	200		11,515		Ltd(Refund			
1 June	H Stanton plc			8,260		of over-			
1 June	York Jewellers	64		3,136		payment)			
					1 June	Balances c/d		80	29,671
		264	80	29,771				80	29,771

Balances

The following balances are available to you at the start of the day on 1 June 20X7.

	£
Credit customers	
Bijoux Ltd	11,715
Gee & Law Ltd (credit balance)	100
J Llewellyn & Sons Ltd	4,520
H Stanton plc	18,900
York Jewellers	6,300
Sales ledger control	86,200
Sales	980,000
Sales returns	12,630
Discounts allowed	13,100
VAT (credit balance)	16,350

Journal entries

The following items will need to be entered in JLW Ltd's Journal.

1   *Correction of errors*

    (a) A payment for £7,050 to TPA Bullion plc, a credit supplier, has been debited to the account of TP Bullock plc.

    (b) Bank charges of £118 have been debited to the interest received account instead of being debited to the bank charges account.

2   A polishing machine has been purchased for £470, inclusive of VAT at 17.5%, on 30 days credit from Excel Machines Ltd.

Trial run central assessments

SECTION 1: PROCESSING EXERCISE (Suggested time allocation: 90 minutes)

COMPLETE ALL FIVE TASKS

Task 1 Enter the opening balances listed on page 103 into the following accounts, which are provided on pages 104 to 107.

Bijoux Ltd
Gee & Law Ltd
J Llewellyn & Sons Ltd
H Stanton plc
York Jewellers
Sales ledger control
Sales
Sales returns
Discounts allowed
VAT

Task 2 Using the data shown on page 102, enter all the transactions into the accounts listed in Task 1.

Task 3 Balance off all the accounts on pages 104 to 107, clearly showing the balances carried down.

Task 4 Using the journal page provided on page 108, record the journal entries above.

Note. Narratives are not required in the journal. The journal items are *not* to be entered in the accounts on pages 104 to 107.

Task 5 Complete the trial balance on page 109 by inserting the figure for each account in either the debit column or the credit column. Ignore the journal items in Task 4 for this purpose. The two totals should be the same. If they do not agree, try to trace and correct any errors you have made within the time available. If you are still unable to make the totals balance, leave the work incomplete.

SALES LEDGER

Bijoux Ltd

Date	Details	Amount £	Date	Details	Amount £

Gee and Law Ltd

Date	Details	Amount £	Date	Details	Amount £

J Llewellyn & Sons Ltd

Date	Details	Amount £	Date	Details	Amount £

H Stanton plc

Date	Details	Amount £	Date	Details	Amount £

Trial run central assessments

York Jewellers

Date	Details	Amount £	Date	Details	Amount £

GENERAL LEDGER

Sales Ledger Control

Date	Details	Amount £	Date	Details	Amount £

Sales

Date	Details	Amount £	Date	Details	Amount £

Sales Returns

Date	Details	Amount £	Date	Details	Amount £

Discounts Allowed

Date	Details	Amount £	Date	Details	Amount £

VAT

Date	Details	Amount £	Date	Details	Amount £

JOURNAL			
Date	Details	Debit	Credit

UPDATED TRIAL BALANCE

	Debit balances £	Credit balances £
Sales ledger control		
Sales		
Sales returns		
Discounts allowed		
VAT		
Other debit balances	1,416,059	
Other credit balances		508,828
Totals		

Trial run central assessments

SECTION 2: TASKS AND QUESTIONS (Suggested time allocation: 90 mins)

Write in the space provided *or* circle the correct answer. Do *not* indicate your answer in any other way. Answer *all* the following tasks and questions.

1 The following invoice, relating to the redecoration of a retail property, has been received by JLW Ltd.

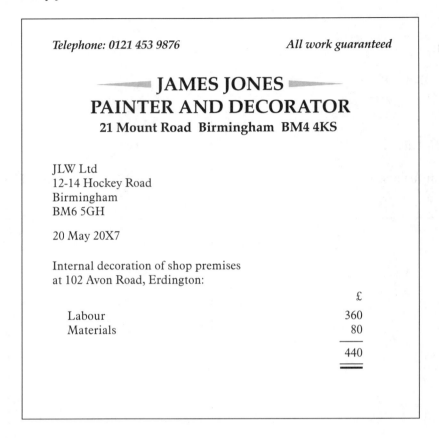

Prepare the cheque provided below to pay the above invoice.

2   (a) JLW Ltd has taken out a bank loan, which is to be repaid over a two year period by eight equal quarterly repayments.

Which service provided by the banks would seem most appropriate for these payments?

....

(b) What is a post-dated cheque?

....

3   Would the following errors cause a difference between the balance of the sales ledger control account and the total of the balances in the sales ledger?

(a) The sales returns day book has been undercast by £10.

Yes/No

(b) A credit note issued to Midgems Ltd for £32 has been credited to the account of Middletons Ltd.

Yes/No

(c) One of the sales ledger accounts has been balanced off incorrectly.

Yes/No

4   (a) What entries are required in the *general ledger* to record the return of goods costing £235, inclusive of 17½% VAT, to a credit supplier?

Debit	Amount £	Credit	Amount £
....	....	....	....
....	....	....	....

(b) JLW Ltd has sold a selection of gold bracelets to a credit customer for a total price (exclusive of VAT) of £2,600. A settlement (cash) discount of 2% is offered for payment within seven days.

Calculate the VAT which must be charged on this sale.

....

....

(c) Should the total of the VAT column in the petty cash book be debited or credited to the VAT account?

Debited/Credited

5   JLW Ltd only accepts cheques supported by a guarantee card. A retail customer wants to pay by cheque for a ring costing £160. The customer has a cheque guarantee card with a limit of £100 and offers to make out one cheque for £100 and another one for £60.

(a) Should you accept the two cheques in payment for the ring?

Yes/No

(b) Explain briefly the reasons for your answer.

....

....

6   What is the purpose of a proforma invoice?

    ....

    ....

7   JLW Ltd pays electricity and gas bills by direct debit, which the bank operates through BACS.

    What do the initials BACS stand for?

    ....

8   What do the following initials represent?

    (a) VDU ....

    (b) RAM ....

    (c) ROM ....

9   JLW Ltd has extracted the following summary figures for wages and salaries for the month of June.

	£
Gross pay	17,790
Tax	2,847
Employees' NIC	1,407
Employer's NIC	1,629
Net pay	13,536

    Task

    Prepare and total the wages control account shown below.

    WAGES CONTROL ACCOUNT

Date 20X0	Details	Amount £	Date 20X0	Details	Amount £

10

STOCK CONTROL

Date	Details	£	Date	Details	£
1 March	Balance b/f	15,000			

This is the stock control account of JLW Ltd. However, a recent physical stock check revealed goods in stock totalled £14,600. What may have caused this difference to occur?

ROUGH WORK

TRIAL RUN CENTRAL ASSESSMENT 2

FOUNDATION STAGE
REVISED STANDARDS
NVQ/SVQ LEVEL 2 IN ACCOUNTING

Preparing Ledger Balances
and an Initial Trial Balance

The Central Assessment is in two parts.

Section 1   Processing Exercise
             Complete all 5 tasks

Section 2   Ten Tasks and Questions
             Complete all tasks and questions

**DO NOT OPEN THIS PAPER UNTIL YOU ARE READY TO START
UNDER TIMED CONDITIONS**

Trial run central assessments

You are reminded that competence must be achieved in each section You should therefore attempt and aim to complete EVERY task in BOTH sections. All essential workings should be included within your answers where appropriate

You are advised to spend 90 minutes on Section 1 and 90 minutes on Section 2.

INTRODUCTION

- Hathaway Design & Print is a family business offering printing services to industry.
- The Chief Accountant is Susan Hathaway.
- You are an Accounting Technician employed to assist Susan Hathaway.
- Double entry takes place in the nominal (general) ledger and the individual accounts of debtors and creditors are therefore regarded as memoranda accounts.

DATA

Transactions

The following transactions, which occurred on 1 June 20X8, have been recorded in the Sales Day Book and the Cash Book (given below) but have not yet been entered into the ledger system. VAT has been calculated at a rate of 17½ %.

SALES DAY BOOK

Date	Details	Invoice No.	Gross	VAT	Net
20X8			£	£	£
1 June	H Booth Limited	HO1972	1,692	252	1,440
1 June	W Dalton Limited	HO1973	752	112	640
1 June	The Peters Partnership	HO1974	2,350	350	2,000
1 June	H Booth Limited	HO1975	2,021	301	1,720
1 June	T Burbridge Limited	HO1976	470	70	400
1 June	W Dalton Limited	HO1977	94	14	80
	Totals		7,379	1,099	6,280

CASH BOOK

Date		Discount Allowed	Cash	Bank	Date	Details	Discount received	Cash	Bank
20X8		£	£	£			£	£	£
1 June	Balance b/f		120	8,392	1 June	Motor vehicle purchase			14,500
1 June	H Booth Limited	200		2,350	1 June	Loan repayment			450
1 June	T Burbridge Limited			940	1 June	Bank charges			108
1 June	W Dalton Limited			15,275	1 June	Motor insurance			317
					1 June	Balances c/f		120	11,582
		200	120	26,957				120	26,957

Balances

The following balances are available to you at the start of the day on 1 June 20X8:

	£
Credit customers	
H Booth Limited	8,225
T Burbridge Limited	7,050
The Peters Partnership	5,875
W Dalton Limited	29,375
Sales	726,506
Sales (Debtors) ledger control	162,150
Bank charges	967
Discount Allowed	370
VAT (credit balance)	15,365
Bank loan	15,300
Motor vehicles	17,650
Motor insurance	495

Journal entries

The following errors have been discovered and will need to be entered in Hathaway Design & Print's journal:

1. An amount of £717 has been recorded in the Office Equipment account instead of in the Electricity account.

2. A payment of £470 from a credit customer, Belton & Byng Limited, has been entered in the account of another credit customer, Belton Stationers, in error.

Trial run central assessments

SECTION 1: PROCESSING EXERCISE (Suggested time allocation: 90 minutes)

COMPLETE ALL THE FOLLOWING TASKS

Task 1 Enter the opening balances listed on page 117 into the following accounts, which are provided on pages 119-121.

> H Booth Limited
> T Burbridge Limited
> The Peters Partnership
> W Dalton Limited
> Sales
> Sales (Debtors) Ledger Control
> Bank Charges
> Discounts Allowed
> VAT
> Bank Loan
> Motor Vehicles
> Motor Insurance

Task 2 Using the data shown on pages 116 and 117, enter all the transactions into the relevant accounts.

Task 3 Balance off all the accounts *clearly showing the balances carried down.*

Task 4 Using the journal page provided on page 122 record the journal entries listed on page 117.

> NB
> - Narratives are not required in the journal.
> - Journal items are NOT to be entered in the accounts.

Task 5 Complete the trial balance on page 123 by inserting the figure for each account in either the debit column or the credit column. Ignore the journal items in Task 4 for this purpose. The two totals should be the same. If they do not agree, try to trace and correct any errors you have made within the time available. If you are still unable to make the totals balance, leave the work incomplete.

SALES LEDGER

H Booth Limited

Date	Details	Amount	Date	Details	Amount
		£			£

T Burbridge Limited

Date	Details	Amount	Date	Details	Amount
		£			£

The Peters Partnership

Date	Details	Amount	Date	Details	Amount
		£			£

W Dalton Limited

Date	Details	Amount	Date	Details	Amount
		£			£

GENERAL (MAIN) LEDGER

Sales

Date	Details	Amount £	Date	Details	Amount £

Sales (Debtors) Ledger Control

Date	Details	Amount £	Date	Details	Amount £

Bank Charges

Date	Details	Amount £	Date	Details	Amount £

Discounts Allowed

Date	Details	Amount £	Date	Details	Amount £

VAT

Date	Details	Amount £	Date	Details	Amount £

Bank Loan

Date	Details	Amount £	Date	Details	Amount £

Motor Vehicles

Date	Details	Amount £	Date	Details	Amount £

Motor Insurance

Date	Details	Amount £	Date	Details	Amount £

Trial run central assessments

JOURNAL

Date	Details	Debit £	Credit £

UPDATED TRIAL BALANCE

	Debit balances	Credit balances
	£	£
Sales		
Sales (debtors) ledger control		
Bank charges		
Discount allowed		
VAT		
Bank loan		
Motor vehicles		
Motor insurance		
Other debit balances	588,964	
Other credit balances		10,235
Totals		

Trial run central assessments

SECTION 2: TASKS AND QUESTIONS (Suggested time allocation: 90 minutes)

Write in the space provided *or* circle the correct answer. Do *not* indicate your choice in any other way. Answer *all* the following tasks and questions.

1   A petty cash control account is kept in the main (general) ledger of Hathaway Design and Print. The petty cash book is the subsidiary account. At the beginning of January there is a balance brought forward of £350.

During January £250 was spent from petty cash, and at the end of the month, £300 was put into the petty cash box from the bank.

Task

Enter these transactions into the petty cash control account below, showing clearly the balance carried down.

PETTY CASH CONTROL ACCOUNT

Date 20X1	Details	£	Date 20X1	Details	£

2   (a)   What entries are required in the *general (main) ledger* to write off a bad debt of £352.50, inclusive of VAT at 17½%? The VAT can be reclaimed.

Dr	£	*Cr*	£
....	....	....	....
....	....	....	....
....	....	....	....
....	....	....	....

(b)   Briefly explain why a business would try to keep the amount of bad debts written off to a minimum.

....
....
....

(c)   What is the purpose of the following documents?

(i)   Delivery note ....
....
....

(ii)   Goods received note..
....
....

(iii) Advice note ....
....
....

3   What do you understand by the term *personal account* within an accounting system?

    ....
    ....
    ....

4   Give *three* reasons why the balance on Hathaway Design & Print's bank statement may not agree with the balance in its cash book.

    ....
    ....
    ....

5   A cheque for £600 was received from a customer to Hathaway Design & Print but the customer's bank has now returned the cheque marked 'refer to drawer'.

    What does this action usually indicate?

    ....
    ....
    ....

6   Hathaway Design & Print has recently bought a new printing machine. Would the following be capital or revenue expenditure?

    (a) Purchase of the printing machine

        Capital / Revenue

    (b) Substantial staff training costs to operate the pricing machine.

        Capital / Revenue

    (c) Ink for the printing machine

        Capital / Revenue

7   Give *two* advantages of a computerised accounting system.

    ....
    ....

8   Would you find the following accounts in the general (main) ledger, purchases ledger or sales ledger?

    (a) Creditors control account ....
    (b) Sales returns account ....
    (c) B Cox Limited (a supplier) ....

Trial run central assessments

9   Hathaway Design & Print keeps petty cash in a plastic bag on a shelf in the office so that it is convenient for everyone to access. Make *two* suggestions to improve security.

    ....

    ....

    ....

10 **STOCK CONTROL**

Date	Details	£	Date	Details	£
1 March	Balance b/f	38,000			

This is the stock control account of Hathaway Designs and Print. However, a recent physical stock check revealed goods in stock totalled £37,900. What may have caused this difference to occur?

ROUGH WORK

AAT SPECIMEN CENTRAL ASSESSMENT

FOUNDATION STAGE
REVISED STANDARDS
NVQ/SVQ LEVEL 2 IN ACCOUNTING

Preparing Ledger Balances
and an Initial Trial Balance

The Central Assessment is in two parts.

Section 1   Processing Exercise
            Complete all 5 tasks

Section 2   Ten tasks and questions
            Complete all tasks and questions

DO NOT OPEN THIS PAPER UNTIL YOU ARE READY TO START UNDER TIMED CONDITIONS

AAT Specimen central assessment

You are reminded that competence must be achieved in each section You should therefore attempt and aim to complete EVERY task in BOTH sections.

All essential workings should be included within your answers where appropriate

You are advised to spend 90 minutes on Section 1 and 90 minutes on Section 2.

The central assessment is in two sections.

Section 1　　　　Processing Exercise
　　　　　　　　Complete all five tasks

Section 2　　　　Ten tasks and questions
　　　　　　　　Complete all tasks and questions

Sections 1 and 2 both relate to the company described below.

INTRODUCTION

- Amy McInnes is the owner of a business which supplies office stationery, office equipment and printed brochures
- The business' name is Paperstop.
- You are employed by the company as a bookkeeper
- Double entry takes place in the main (general) ledger and the individual accounts of debtors and creditors are therefore regarded as memorandum accounts.
- Assume today's date is 31 May 20X0.

DATA

Transactions

The following transactions all occurred on 31 May 20X0 and have been entered into the relevant books of prime entry (given below). No entries have yet been made into the ledger system. VAT has been calculated at the rate of 17½%.

SALES DAY BOOK

Date 20X0	Details	Invoice No	Total	VAT	Net
31 May	HTP Ltd	756	1,175	175	1,000
31 May	B Avery & Company	757	1,880	280	1,600
31 May	Garners Ltd	758	1,645	245	1,400
31 May	Rowley & Rudge	759	2,350	350	2,000
	Totals		7,050	1,050	6,000

SALES RETURNS DAY BOOK

Date 20X0	Details	Credit Note No	Total £	VAT £	Net £
31 May	HTP Ltd	CR18	235	35	200
31 May	Rowley & Rudge	CR19	141	21	120
	Totals		376	56	320

CASH BOOK

Date 20X0	Details	Discount allowed	Bank £	Date 20X0	Details	Discount received	Bank £
31 May	Balance b/f		3,600	31 May	Motor tax		90
31 May	B Avery & Co	100	3,900	31 May	Charitable donation		50
31 May	Rowley & Rudge		1,000	31 May	Bank charges		156
				31 May	Balance c/d		8,204
		100	8,500				8,500

BALANCES TO BE INSERTED INTO LEDGER ACCOUNTS

The following balances are relevant to you at the start of the day on 31 May 20X0.

	£
Credit customers	
HTP Ltd	8,300
B Avery & Company	4,400
Garners Ltd	1,850
Rudge and Rowley	4,700
Sales	225,185
Sales returns	1,080
Debtors control	63,816
Bank charges	100
Discounts allowed	700
Motor tax and insurance	180
VAT (credit balance)	11,198

BALANCES TO BE TRANSFERRED TO TRIAL BALANCE

	£
Motor vehicles	28,300
Office equipment	7,000
Stock	35,587
Cash	75
Creditors control	34,880
Capital	16,723
Purchases	101,857
Purchases returns	366
Discounts received	132
Wages	37,843
Rent and rates	4,000
Electricity	814
Telephone	922
Motor fuel	780
Miscellaneous expenses	1,830

AAT Specimen central assessment

SECTION 1: PROCESSING EXERCISE

(Suggested time allocation 90 minutes)

Blank space for workings is available on page 142

Task 1.1 Enter the opening balances listed on page 131 into the following accounts, which are provided on pages 133-135:

    HTP Ltd
    B Avery & Company
    Garners Ltd
    Rowley & Rudge
    Sales
    Sales returns
    Debtors control
    Bank charges
    Discounts allowed
    Motor tax and insurance
    VAT

Task 1.2 From the day books and cash book shown on pages 130 and 131 make the relevant entries into the accounts in the subsidiary (sales) ledger and main (general) ledger.

Task 1.3 Balance off all of the accounts *showing clearly the balances carried down.*

Task 1.4 Transfer the balances calculated in Task 1.3 and from the cash book to the relevant columns of the trial balance shown on page 136.

Task 1.5 Transfer the remaining balances shown on page 131 to the trial balance and total each column. The debit column and credit column totals should be the same.

Task 1.1, 1.2 and 1.3

SUBSIDIARY (SALES) LEDGER

HTP Limited

Date	Details	Amount £	Date	Details	Amount £

B Avery & Company

Date	Details	Amount £	Date	Details	Amount £

Garners Limited

Date	Details	Amount £	Date	Details	Amount £

Rowley & Rudge

Date	Details	Amount £	Date	Details	Amount £

MAIN (GENERAL) LEDGER

Sales

Date	Details	Amount £	Date	Details	Amount £

Sales returns

Date	Details	Amount £	Date	Details	Amount £

Debtors control

Date	Details	Amount £	Date	Details	Amount £

Bank charges

Date	Details	Amount £	Date	Details	Amount £

Discounts allowed

Date	Details	Amount £	Date	Details	Amount £

Motor tax and insurance

Date	Details	Amount £	Date	Details	Amount £

Charitable donations

Date	Details	Amount £	Date	Details	Amount £

VAT

Date	Details	Amount £	Date	Details	Amount £

AAT Specimen central assessment

Task 1.4 and 1.5

TRIAL BALANCE AS AT 31 MAY 20X0

	Debit £	Credit £
Motor vehicle	....	....
Office equipment	....	....
Stock	....	....
Bank	....	....
Cash	....	....
Debtors control	....	....
Creditors control	....	....
VAT	....	....
Capital	....	....
Sales	....	....
Sales returns	....	....
Purchases	....	....
Purchases returns	....	....
Bank charges	....	....
Discounts allowed	....	....
Discounts received	....	....
Wages	....	....
Rent and rates	....	....
Electricity	....	....
Telephone	....	....
Motor tax and insurance	....	....
Motor fuel	....	....
Charitable donations	....	....
Miscellaneous expenses	....	....
Total	....	....

WORKINGS

AAT Specimen central assessment

SECTION 2: TASKS AND QUESTIONS

(Suggested time allocation: 90 minutes)

Write in the space provided OR circle the correct answer. Do not indicate your choice in any other way

ANSWER ALL OF THE FOLLOWING TASKS AND QUESTIONS

2.1 Complete the paying-in slip and counterfoil below to bank the cash that Paperstop has in its safe today.

One	£20 note	Four	50p coins
Three	£10 notes	Ten	20p coins
Three	£5 notes	Twelve	10p coins
Four	£1 coins	Forty	2p coins

2.2 Paperstop is considering using an analysed sales day book and sales returns day book. **Suggest THREE ways in which Paperstop may wish to analyse its sales.**

....
....
....
....

2.3 **Name THREE items of capital expenditure and THREE items of revenue expenditure that Paperstop is likely to incur.**

Capital expenditure   Revenue expenditure

....
....
....

2.4 Paperstop operates a monthly payroll system and all of the payroll figures pass through a wages and salaries control accounts. **Name FOUR entries you would expect to see in the wages and salaries control account.**

....
....
....
....

2.5 Complete the following sentences.

(a) Paperstop sends out a..
to inform the customer that its order has been received and is being dealt with.

(b) Paperstop sends out an..
to inform the customer when the goods on order will be delivered.

(c) Paperstop sends out a..
to request payment BEFORE goods are delivered.

(d) Paperstop raises a..
to record the receipt of goods into its warehouse.

2.6 Paperstop has always filed its correspondence with customers and suppliers in date order, but as the business has grown this system is no longer effective. **Suggest ONE method of filing correspondence which would be more appropriate.**

....
....

2.7 The following errors and adjustments are to be corrected in Paperstop's accounting records.

(a) An amount of £100.00 has been credited to the bank charges paid account instead of the bank interest received account.

(b) An amount of £34.00 has been debited to the motor fuel account and the same amount credited to the bank account, instead of the correct figure of £43.00.

(c) A credit customer, Gee & Company, has ceased trading and the amount outstanding on its account of £600 plus VAT is to be written off as a bad debt.

Complete the journal entries required to correct the above errors.

Note. You are NOT required to make any adjustments to the accounts in Section 1. No narratives are required.

Date	Details	Dr	Cr

2.8 The creditors control account has a credit balance of £34,880 as at 31 May 20X0. **Confirm the accuracy of this figure by completing the document below using the following information.**

	£
Balance of creditors control account as at 1 May 20X0	37,612
Purchase invoices received in May	5,413
Purchase credit notes received in May	874
Payments made in May	6,981
Discounts received in May	290

CREDITORS CONTROL ACCOUNT CHECK AS AT 31 MAY 20X0

	£	£
Balance as at 1 May 20X0		....
Purchases invoices received	....	
Purchases credit notes received	....	
Payments made	....	
Discounts received	....	
		....
Balance as at 31 May 20X0		_____

2.9 Give TWO reasons for maintaining a creditors control account.

....

....

....

2.10 Paperstop has received the following bank statement as at 30 May 20X0 which you are to check against the cash book shown below.

(a) **Check the items on the bank statement against the items in the cash book and update the cash book accordingly. Total the cash book and clearly show the balance carried down.**

Note. None of the details below are relevant to Section 1.

LOWLANDS BANK plc
15 George Street, Nottingham, NG11 8TU

To: Paperstop   Account No 31176786   30 May 20X0

STATEMENT OF ACCOUNT

DATE	DETAILS	DEBIT	CREDIT	BALANCE
20X0		£	£	£
1 May	Balance b/f			1,181
5 May	Cheque No 198470	100		1,081
5 May	Credit		480	1,561
8 May	Bank Giro Credit Bakers Ltd		3,000	4,561
10 May	Cheque No 198471	235		4,326
16 May	Direct debit Keen & Co	850		3,476
24 May	Bank charges	56		3,420
25 May	Direct debit Cox Cleaning	150		3,270
30 May	Cheque No 198473	80		3,190

D = Debit   C = Credit

CASH BOOK

Date 20X0	Details	Amount £	Date 20X0	Details	Amount £
1 May	Balance b/f	1,181	1 May	Downing & co	100
1 May	B King	480	5 May	GPT Ltd	235
24 May	C West	8,000	12 May	H&L Insurers	6,821
25 May	L Kingsley	1,175	23 May	Conners Ltd	80

(b) **Give THREE reasons why the balance in the cash book does not match the closing balance on the bank statement.**

....

....

....

DECEMBER 2000 CENTRAL ASSESSMENT

FOUNDATION STAGE
REVISED STANDARDS
NVQ/SVQ LEVEL 2 IN ACCOUNTING

Preparing Ledger Balances
and an Initial Trial Balance

The Central Assessment is in two parts.

Section 1   Processing Exercise
Complete all 5 tasks

Section 2   Ten Tasks and Questions
Complete all tasks and questions

DO NOT OPEN THIS PAPER UNTIL YOU ARE READY TO START UNDER TIMED CONDITIONS

December 2000 central assessment

You must show competence in each section. Attempt, and aim to complete, EVERY task in EACH section.

Include all essential workings within your answers, where appropriate.

This Central Assessment is in two sections. You should spend 90 minutes on each section.

Section 1 Processing exercise
Complete all five tasks

Section 2 10 tasks and questions
Complete all tasks and questions

INTRODUCTION

- Paul Province is the owner of Pots and Pans, a business that supplies cooking utensils to the catering industry.

- You are employed by the business as a bookkeeper.

- The business operates a manual accounting system.

- Double entry takes place in the main (general) ledger. Individual accounts of debtors and creditors are kept in subsidiary ledgers as memorandum accounts.

- Assume today's date is 30 November 20X0

DATA

The following balances are relevant to you at the start of the day on 30 November 20X0.

	£
Credit customers	
Cooks Company	10,575
Bakers Dozen	5,875
Pastry Case Ltd	11,750
Greenwoods Pies	1,250
Sales	309,000
Sales returns	2,968
Debtors control	106,840
Bank charges	367
Discounts allowed	170
Insurance	600
Rent paid	850
VAT (credit balance)	16,512

December 2000 central assessment

SECTION 1 – PROCESSING EXERCISE (Suggested time allocation: 90 mins)

COMPLETE ALL THE FOLLOWING TASKS

Task 1.1 Enter these opening balances into the following accounts given on pages 147 to 149.

Subsidiary (sales) ledger
- Cooks Company
- Bakers Dozen
- Pastry Case Ltd
- Greenwoods Pies

Main (general) ledger
- Sales
- Sales returns
- Debtors control
- Bank charges
- Discounts allowed
- Insurance
- Rent paid
- VAT

DATA

The following transactions all occurred on 30 November 20X0 and have been entered into the relevant books of prime entry as shown below. No entries have yet been made into the ledger system The VAT rate is 17½%.

SALES DAY BOOK

Date 20X0	Details	Invoice no	Total £	VAT £	Net £
30 Nov	Cooks Company	8321	2,115	315	1,800
30 Nov	Bakers Dozen	8322	940	140	800
30 Nov	Pastry Case Ltd	8323	8,225	1,225	7,000
30 Nov	Greenwoods Pies	8324	705	105	600
	Totals		11,985	1,785	10,200

SALES RETURNS DAY BOOK

Date 20X0	Details	Credit note no	Total £	VAT £	Net £
30 Nov	Bakers Dozen	CR23	470	70	400
30 Nov	Pastry Case Ltd	CR24	1,175	175	1,000
	Totals		1,645	245	1,400

CASH BOOK

Date 20X0	Details	Discount allowed	Bank £	Date 20X0	Details	Discount received	Bank £
30 Nov	Balance b/f		2,700	30 Nov	Bank charges		87
30 Nov	Cooks Company	50	1,950	30 Nov	Insurance		700
30 Nov	Greenwoods Pies		750	30 Nov	Rent paid		300
				30 Nov	Balance c/f		4,313
	Totals	50	5,400				5,400

Task 1.2 From the day books and cash book shown above, make the relevant entries into the accounts in the subsidiary (sales) ledger, page 147 and main (general) ledger, pages 148 and 149.

Task 1.3 Balance the accounts *showing clearly the balances carried down.*

Task 1.4 Transfer the balances calculated in Task 1.3, and the bank balance, to the trial balance on page 151.

SUBSIDIARY (SALES) LEDGER

COOKS COMPANY

Date	Details	Amount £	Date	Details	Amount £

BAKERS DOZEN

Date	Details	Amount £	Date	Details	Amount £

PASTRY CASE LIMITED

Date	Details	Amount £	Date	Details	Amount £

GREENWOODS PIES

Date	Details	Amount £	Date	Details	Amount £

MAIN (GENERAL) LEDGER

SALES

Date	Details	Amount £	Date	Details	Amount £

SALES RETURNS

Date	Details	Amount £	Date	Details	Amount £

DEBTORS CONTROL

Date	Details	Amount £	Date	Details	Amount £

BANK CHARGES

Date	Details	Amount £	Date	Details	Amount £

MAIN (GENERAL) LEDGER, CONTINUED

DISCOUNTS ALLOWED

Date	Details	Amount £	Date	Details	Amount £

INSURANCE

Date	Details	Amount £	Date	Details	Amount £

RENT PAID

Date	Details	Amount £	Date	Details	Amount £

VAT

Date	Details	Amount £	Date	Details	Amount £

December 2000 central assessment

DATA

Other balances to be transferred to the trial balance:

	£
Motor vehicles	37,200
Office equipment	9,700
Stock	56,540
Cash	190
Creditors control	47,910
Capital	19,381
Purchases	126,003
Purchases returns	459
Commission paid	890
Wages	42,078
Rates	1,200
Electricity	981
Telephone	1,585
Motor expenses	900
Miscellaneous expenses	1,500

Task 1.5 Transfer the remaining balances shown above to the trial balance on page 151 and total each column.

TRIAL BALANCE AS AT 30 NOVEMBER 20X0

	Debit £	Credit £
Motor vehicles	....	....
Office equipment	....	....
Stock	....	....
Bank	....	....
Cash	....	....
Debtors control	....	....
Creditors control	....	....
VAT	....	....
Capital	....	....
Sales	....	....
Sales returns	....	....
Purchases	....	....
Purchases returns	....	....
Commission paid	....	....
Bank charges	....	....
Discounts allowed	....	....
Wages	....	....
Insurance	....	....
Rent paid	....	....
Rates	....	....
Electricity	....	....
Telephone	....	....
Motor expenses	....	....
Miscellaneous expenses	....	....
Total	=======	=======

December 2000 central assessment

SECTION 2 – TASKS AND QUESTIONS (Suggested time allocation: 90 mins)

Task 2.1 You received this cheque today

```
MBC Bank                                      40-30-23
1 Aston Road                    Date    23 Nov 20W9
Birmingham B8 91A

Pay   Pots and Pans
      Seven hundred and five pounds      £  750.00
                                         M Gray & Company
100659 II 90 III 3023 IIII 62359802
```

(a) Give *three* reasons why the bank will not honour the cheque.

....

....

....

....

(b) What would you do in this situation?

....

....

....

....

Task 2.2 Pots and Pans wants to computerise all of its recording systems.

(a) Give three advantages to Pots and Pans of computerising its accounting system.

....

....

....

....

(b) A computerised accounting system is one example of a data recording system. Give *one* other example.

....

....

Task 2.3 Give *two* reasons for producing a trial balance.

....

....

....

....

Task 2.4 The cash book is written up from source documents, such as cheque book counterfoils.

Name *two* other source documents which would be used to make entries into the cash book.

....

....

....

....

Task 2.5 What document would Pots and Pans send out?

(a) To remind customers of their outstanding account and request payment each month

....

(b) To record the return of goods from a customer

....

(c) To be signed by a customer as proof of delivery of goods

....

(d) To let customers know when their goods will be delivered

....

Task 2.6 Pots and Pans has a policy of banking all cheques and cash at the end of every working day.

(a) Give *two* reasons why Pots and Pans pays into the bank every working day.

....

....

(b) Name *one* service that banks offer which would help Pots and Pans if it was not possible to take the cash to the bank before closing time.

....

....

Task 2.7 Your work at Pots and Pans is highly confidential.

Name *two* actions you would take to ensure the security and confidentiality of information.

....

....

....

Task 2.8 Entries need to be made in the accounting records of Pots and Pans for the following.

(a) £90.00 has been debited to the rent paid account instead of the rates account.

(b) £69.00 has been debited to the commission paid account and credited to the bank account instead of the correct amount of £96.00.

(c) A credit customer, Crusty Cobs Ltd, has ceased trading. The amount outstanding on its account of £800.00 plus VAT is to be written off as a bad debt.

Complete the journal entries necessary to record the above in the main (general) ledger. Narratives are not required.

Note. You do *not* need to adjust accounts in Section 1.

Date	Details	Dr	Cr

Task 2.9 (a) The following transactions with suppliers took place in November.

	£
Purchased goods on credit	11,750
Paid creditors	2,833
Discounts received	406
Returned goods to suppliers	704

The balance of creditors at 1 November was £40,103.

Prepare a creditors control account from the above details, showing clearly the balance carried down.

CREDITORS CONTROL

Date	Details	Amount £	Date	Details	Amount £

(b) The following balances were shown in the subsidiary (purchases) ledger on 30 November. Reconcile these balances with the creditors control account balance you calculated on page 155.

	£
Byng & Company	13,058 Credit
LTF Ltd	11,870 Credit
Derby & White	10,410 Credit
A & B Ltd	3,800 Credit
Condor Ltd	100 Debit
Cartwright Ltd	5,601 Credit
Three Sisters Trading	3,071 Credit

	£
Creditors control account balance as at 30 November 20X0	
Total of subsidiary (purchases) ledger accounts as at 30 November 20X0	
Difference	

(c) What do you think may have caused the difference calculated in (b)?

....

....

....

Task 2.10 On 3 December Pots and Pans received the following bank statement as at 30 November 20X0 which you are to check against the cash book shown below.

Note. None of the details below is relevant to Section 1.

(a) Check the items on the bank statement against the items in the cash book and update the cash book accordingly. Total the cash book and clearly show the balance carried down.

CENTRE POINT BANK plc
High Street, Little Heath, Birmingham, B72 1AD

To: Pots and Pans Account No 46138291 30 November 20X0

STATEMENT OF ACCOUNT

DATE 20X0	DETAILS	DEBIT £	CREDIT £	BALANCE £
1 Nov	Balance b/f			2,626 C
5 Nov	Cheque No 218465	58		2,568 C
5 Nov	Credit		580	3,148 C
8 Nov	Bank Giro Credit Creamy Cakes		6,600	9,748 C
10 Nov	Cheque No 218467	8,000		1,748 C
16 Nov	Direct debit B A Roberts Ltd	1,400		348 C
24 Nov	Bank charges	108		240 C
25 Nov	Direct debit Land Security	200		40 C
30 Nov	Cheque No 218468	540		500 D

CASH BOOK

Date 20X0	Details	Bank £	Date 20X0	Cheque No	Details	Bank £
1 Nov	Balance b/f	2,626	1 Nov	218465	Byng & Company	58
1 Nov	L Weston	580	5 Nov	218466	LTF Ltd	470
24 Nov	B Carter	2,350	12 Nov	218467	P&S Insurance	8,000
25 Nov	C Keats	7,990	23 Nov	218468	Derby & white	540
			29 Nov	218469	The Flour Mill	705

(b) Using the data above, give four reasons why the balance in your updated cash book does not match the closing balance on the bank statement

....

....

....

....

....

Answers to practice activities

CHAPTER 1: REVISION OF BASIC BOOKKEEPING

1 STOCK OR ASSET

(a) Capital
(b) Revenue

2 ADVICE NOTE

False

3 REDECORATION

(a) Revenue
(b) Capital

4 REMITTANCE ADVICE

False

5 BUSINESS DOCUMENTATION

(a) Monthly statement of account
(b) Credit note
(c) Purchase order

Answers to practice activities

CHAPTER 2: RECORDING, SUMMARISING AND POSTING TRANSACTIONS

6 WHICH LEDGER?

(a) Main ledger
(b) Main ledger
(c) Main ledger

7 DELIVERY VAN

(a) No

(b) The amount of money kept in petty cash should be kept to a minimum to prevent fraud and theft. The amount would be far too large to keep in petty cash.

8 CLASSIFYING ACCOUNTS

(a) Expense
(b) Revenue
(c) Asset
(d) Liability
(e) Expense

9 ENTRIES

(a) A credit note

(b)

			£	£
DEBIT	Sales		78.30	
	VAT		13.70	
CREDIT	Debtors control account			92.00

10 WHEREABOUTS

(a) Purchase ledger
(b) Main ledger
(c) Main ledger

11 MAIN LEDGER ENTRIES

		£	£
DEBIT	VAT	28	
DEBIT	Returns inwards	160	
CREDIT	Creditors control		188
DEBIT	VAT	28	
DEBIT	Returns outwards	160	
CREDIT	Sales ledger control		188

Answers to practice activities

CHAPTER 3: FROM LEDGER ACCOUNTS TO INITIAL TRIAL BALANCE

12 BATCH PROCESSING

False

13 CALCULATING VAT

	£
Sales (100%)	1,550,000
VAT (17½%)	271,250
Total (117½%)	1,821,250

VAT on purchases = £271,250 − £26,250 = £245,000.

$$\therefore \text{Vatable purchases (including VAT)} = £245,000 \times \frac{117.5}{17.5} = £1,645,000.$$

$$\text{(excluding VAT)} = £245,000 \times \frac{100}{17.5} = £1,400,000.$$

14 MORE VAT

$$\text{Output VAT} = £846 \times \frac{17.5}{117.5} = £126$$

$$\text{Input VAT} = £7.50 \times 80 \times \frac{17.5}{117.5} = £105$$

∴ Amount owing to Customs and Excise = £(126 − 105) = £21

15 CORRECTING ERRORS

(a) DEBIT   VAT   £14
     CREDIT   Creditors control   £14

(b) DEBIT   Discounts allowed   £98
     CREDIT   Discounts received   £98

(c)
			£	£
	DEBIT	Sales	23	
		Purchases	23	
		VAT	8	
	CREDIT	Debtors control		27
		Creditors control		27

163

Answers to practice activities

CHAPTER 4: BANK RECONCILIATIONS

16 STANDING ORDERS

District Council:

DEBIT	Rates account	£140	
CREDIT	Bank account		£140

Friendly Insurance Company:

DEBIT	Insurance account	£80	
CREDIT	Bank account		£80

Telephone Corporation:

DEBIT	Telephone account	£125	
CREDIT	Bank account		£125

17 JOURNALS

		Dr £	Cr £
DEBIT	Bank account	1,245	
CREDIT	Debtors control account		1,245
	Being bank giro credit from Johnson & Co		
DEBIT	Gas account	330	
CREDIT	Bank account		330
	Being direct debit payment to English Gas Co		
DEBIT	Bank charges account	40	
CREDIT	Bank account		40
	Being bank charges for the period		

18 BANK STATEMENT ENTRIES

A cheque for £156.50 was received from a customer and paid into your bank account on 14 January. The cheque then went through the bank clearing system but the bank was unable to clear the cheque either due to the fact that the cheque was not correctly drawn up or the drawee did not have sufficient funds in his account. Therefore the cheque will have been returned to you marked 'refer to drawer'.

The cash book must be amended as it will currently show a receipt for £156.50. However, the money has not been received and therefore a credit entry is needed in the bank account, the payments side of the cash book. The cheque should be returned to the customer with a request for a replacement cheque.

Answers to practice activities

19 UPDATE

(a) and (b)

CASH BOOK							
RECEIPTS				PAYMENTS			
Date	Detail		£	Date	Detail	Cheque no	£
1 June	Balance b/d		572	5 June	J Taylor	013647	334
8 June	Hardy & Co		493	16 June	K Filter	013648	127
12 June	T Roberts		525	22 June	B Gas	013649	200
18 June	D Smith		617	28 June	Wages	BACS	940
25 June	Garnet Bros		369	29 June	D Perez	013650	317
	A Hammond -				Telephone DD		146
4 June	BGC		136	18 June	Balance c/d		659
30 June	Bank interest		11	30 June			
			2,723				2,723

(c) Cheque number 013650 was not written until 29 June and therefore could not possibly reach the supplier, be paid into the supplier's bank account and work its way through the bank clearing system by 30 June.

Cheque number 013648 was written into the cash book on 16 June and therefore theoretically should have cleared through the banking system by the end of the month. However, there may have been a delay in sending the cheque out to the payee or the payee may have delayed in paying the cheque into his bank account meaning that by 30 June the cheque has still not cleared.

20 COMPARE

(a)

CASH BOOK							
RECEIPTS				PAYMENTS			
Date	Detail		£	Date	Detail	Cheque no	£
2 Feb	Davis & Co		183	1 Feb	Balance b/d		306
7 Feb	A Thomas		179	4 Feb	J L Pedro	000351	169
14 Feb	K Sinders		146	11 Feb	P Gecko	000352	104
21 Feb	H Harvey		162	15 Feb	F Dimpner	000353	217
27 Feb	A Watts		180	23 Feb	O Roup	000354	258
				15 Feb	Telephone	SO	65
				24 Feb	Electricity	DD	30
28 Feb	Balance c/d		314	28 Feb	Interest		15
			1,164				1,164

(b) This is a debit balance carried down therefore a credit balance brought down, representing an overdraft. This will appear in the trial balance as a credit balance.

(c) The closing balance on the amended cash book does not agree with the closing bank statement balance for two reasons.

  (i) The cheque received from A Watts for £180 has not yet appeared in the bank statement.

Answers to practice activities

(ii) Cheque number 000354 for £258 has not yet appeared on the bank statement.

21 BALANCE

(a) and (b)

CASH BOOK						
RECEIPTS			PAYMENTS			
Date	*Detail*	*£*	*Date*	*Detail*	*Cheque no*	*£*
1 Jan	Balance b/d	1,035	2 Jan	O J Trading	02475	368
2 Jan	Filter Bros	115	4 Jan	K D Partners	02476	463
8 Jan	Headway Ltd	640	7 Jan	L T Engineers	02477	874
15 Jan	Letterhead Ltd	409	14 Jan	R Trent	02478	315
22 Jan	Leaden Partners	265	20 Jan	I Rain	02479	85
20 Jan	BGC - T Elliot	161	25 Jan	TDC	SO	150
31 Jan	Adjustment to		28 Jan	Wages	02480	490
	cheque no 02477	90	28 Jan	Bank charges		10
31 Jan	Balance c/d	40				
		2,755				2,755

(c) The amended cash book balance does not agree with the bank statement balance at the end of the month due to the fact that cheque numbers 02479 and 02480 have not yet appeared on the bank statement.

CHAPTER 5: STOCK AND BAD DEBTS

22 STOCK CONTROL ACCOUNT 1

- Calculation error in stock record
- Error in physical count of stock
- Error in stock receipt entry on stock record
- Damaged stock
- Theft

23 STOCK CONTROL ACCOUNT 2

- Calculation error in stock record
- Error in physical count of stock
- Error in stock receipt entry on stock record
- Damaged stock
- Theft

24 CASH CONTROL 1

PETTY CASH CONTROL

Date 20X1	Details	£	Date 20X1	Details	£
1 Aug	Balance b/f	175	31 Aug	Petty cash	125
31 Aug	Bank	150	31 Aug	Balance c/d	200
		325			325
1 Sept	Balance b/d	200			

25 CASH CONTROL 2

PETTY CASH CONTROL

Date 20X1	Details	£	Date 20X1	Details	£
1 Jun	Balance b/f	150	30 Jun	Petty cash	100
30 Jun	Bank	200	30 Jun	Balance c/d	250
		350			350
1 July	Balance b/d	250			

26 CASH CONTROL 3

PETTY CASH CONTROL

Date 20X1	Details	£	Date 20X1	Details	£
1 April	Balance b/f	232	30 Apr	Petty cash	210
30 April	Bank	220	30 Apr	Balance c/d	242
		452			452
1 May	Balance b/d	242			

Answers to practice activities

27 WAGES 1

Wages Control Account

Date 20X0	Details	Amount £	Date 20X0	Details	Amount £
30 Sept	Net pay	4,500	30 Sept	Gross wages	6,000
	PAYE	1,100		Employer's NIC	600
	Employees' NIC	400			
	Employer's NIC	600			
		6,600			6,600

28 WAGES 2

Wages Control Account

Date 20X0	Details	Amount £	Date 20X0	Details	Amount £
30 Sept	Net pay	9,000	30 Sept	Gross wages	12,000
	PAYE	2,200		Employer's NIC	1,200
	Employees' NIC	800			
	Employer's NIC	1,200			
		13,200			13,200

29 WAGES 3

Wages Control Account

Date 20X0	Details	Amount £	Date 20X0	Details	Amount £
30 Sept	Net pay	22,500	30 Sept	Gross wages	30,000
	PAYE	5,500		Employer's NIC	3,000
	Employees' NIC	2,000			
	Employer's NIC	3,000			
		33,000			33,000

30 STOCK RECORD CARD 1

STOCK RECORD CARD – DW 156 MULTI-KLEEN DISHWASHER

Date 20X1	Details	In	Out	Quantity in stock	@ £500 per dishwasher £
1 Jan	Opening balance			348	174,000
1 Jan	Sales		20	328	164,000
4 Jan	Sales		40	288	144,000
6 Jan	Sales		100	188	94,000
7 Jan	Sales		30	158	79,000
11 Jan	Sales		40	118	59,000
12 Jan	Faulty		2	116	58,000
13 Jan	Sales		40	76	38,000
15 Jan	Sales		40	36	18,000
18 Jan	Receipt	200		236	118,000
20 Jan	Sales		20	216	108,000
22 Jan	Sales		10	206	103,000
25 Jan	Sales		30	176	88,000
26 Jan	Sales		40	136	68,000
28 Jan	Receipt	220		356	178,000
29 Jan	Sales		40	316	158,000
30 Jan	Sales		40	276	138,000

RECONCILIATION OF STOCK RECORD WITH PHYSICAL STOCK CHECK ON 31 JANUARY 20X1

PHYSICAL STOCK CHECK 278 @ £500	139,000
STORES RECORD CARD QUANTITY	138,000
DIFFERENCE	£1,000

NOTE FOR SUPERVISOR

There is a difference of £1,000 between the value of item DW 156 as reported in the physical stock check and the value on the stores card.

The probable reason for this is the items shown as faulty on 12 January. These may have been included in the stock check by mistake.

Answers to practice activities

31 STOCK RECORD CARD 2

STOCK RECORD CARD – RF 815 REFRESH-KWIK

Date 20X1	Details	In	Out	Quantity in stock	@ £100 per machine £
1 Jan	Opening balance			522	52,200
1 Jan	Sales		30	492	49,200
4 Jan	Sales		60	432	43,200
6 Jan	Sales		150	282	28,200
7 Jan	Sales		45	237	23,700
11 Jan	Sales		60	177	17,700
12 Jan	Faulty		3	174	17,400
13 Jan	Sales		60	114	11,400
15 Jan	Sales		60	54	5,400
18 Jan	Receipt	300		354	35,400
20 Jan	Sales		30	324	32,400
22 Jan	Sales		15	309	30,900
25 Jan	Sales		45	264	26,400
26 Jan	Sales		60	204	20,400
28 Jan	Receipt	330		534	53,400
29 Jan	Sales		60	474	47,400
30 Jan	Sales		60	414	41,400

RECONCILIATION OF STOCK RECORD WITH PHYSICAL STOCK CHECK ON 31 JANUARY 20X1

PHYSICAL STOCK CHECK 417 @ £100	41,700
STORES RECORD CARD QUANTITY	41,400
DIFFERENCE	£300

NOTE FOR SUPERVISOR

There is a difference of £300 between the value of item RF 815 as reported in the physical stock check and the value on the stores card.

The probable reason for this is the items shown as faulty on 12 January. These may have been included in the stock check by mistake.

CHAPTER 6: DEBTORS AND CONTROL ACCOUNTS

32 RECORDING TRANSACTION

(a) DEBIT   Debtors control a/c   £188
    CREDIT   Sales   £160
    CREDIT   VAT   £28

(b) DEBIT   Purchases   £188
    CREDIT   Creditors control a/c   £188

33 ERRORS CAUSE A DIFFERENCE

(a) Yes

(b) No

(c) No. The same mistake would be processed in the sales ledger and the sales ledger control account.

34 SET OFF

DEBIT   Creditors a/c   £75
CREDIT   Debtors control a/c   £75

35 THREE REASONS

(a) To aid in the prevention of fraud
(b) To assist in the location of errors
(c) To enable the total debtors figure to be known at any time

36 DEBTORS CONTROL ACCOUNT RECONCILIATION

DEBTORS CONTROL ACCOUNT

Date 20X0	Details	Amount £	Date 20X0	Details	Amount £
1 August	Balance b/f	182,806	31 August	Sales returns	2,352
31 August	Sales	82,250	31 August	Discounts allowed	100
			31 August	Bank	73,648
			31 August	Balance c/d	188,956
		265,056			265,056
1 Sept	Balance b/d	94,478			

RECONCILIATION OF DEBTORS CONTROL ACCOUNT
WITH SUBIDIARY (SALES) LEDGER
AT 31 AUGUST 20X0

	£
Closing balance of debtors control account	188,956
Total balance of accounts in subsidiary (sales) ledger	188,060
Imbalance	896

Answers to practice activities

> **NOTE TO SUPERVISOR**
>
> There is an imbalance between the debtors control account and subsidiary (sales) ledger of £896. This may be for any number of reasons, but the most likely explanation is that the account of Smith Ltd has a credit balance of £448. We may need to check whether this credit balance ought to be there. Whether the sales ledger or the control account is incorrect, the difference would be £448 × 2, ie £896.

Answers to practice activities

CHAPTER 7: CREDITORS CONTROL ACCOUNT

37 BALANCE OF CCA

(a) Yes
(b) No
(c) No

38 ANOTHER SET OFF

(a) DEBIT   Purchases ledger control a/c   £200
    CREDIT Sales ledger control a/c   £200

(b) DEBIT   Purchase ledger control a/c   £27
    CREDIT Insurance expense   £27

Note. We have assumed that the day book has been posted already to the general ledger.

(c) DEBIT   Stationery   £10
    CREDIT Purchases   £10

39 TRANSACTIONS WITH SUPPLIERS

(a) DEBIT   Fixed assets
    CREDIT Creditors control account

(b) DEBIT   Sales returns
    CREDIT Debtors control account

(b) DEBIT   Creditors control account
    CREDIT Bank

40 MORE DIFFERENCES

(a) No
(b) No
(c) Yes
(d) No

41 CREDITORS CONTROL ACCOUNT RECONCILIATION

CREDITORS CONTROL ACCOUNT

Date 20X0	Details	Amount £	Date 20X0	Details	Amount £
31 Aug	Purchases returns	1,880	1 Aug	Balance b/f	67,200
31 Aug	Discounts received	200	31 Aug	Purchases	63,450
31 Aug	Bank	68,310			
31 Aug	Balance c/d	60,260			
		130,650			130,650
			1 Sept	Balance b/d	60,260

173

Answers to practice activities

RECONCILIATION OF CREDITORS CONTROL ACCOUNT
WITH SUBSIDIARY (PURCHASES) LEDGER
AT 31 AUGUST 20X0

	£
Closing balance of creditors control account	60,260
Total balance of accounts in subsidiary (purchases) ledger	60,260
Imbalance	NIL

CHAPTER 8: FILING

42 DOCUMENTS FOR TRIAL BALANCE

- Cash book
- Bank reconciliation
- Petty cash book
- Reconciliation of petty cash vouchers and cash
- Debtors control account reconciliation
- Creditors control account reconciliation
- Stock count details

43 FILING CORRESPONDENCE

File in alphabetical order of the suppliers' and customers' name.

44 STORAGE

MEMO

To: The owner
From: The bookkeeper
Date: 4 May 20X1
Subject: Confidentiality of ledgers

I have some concerns about the confidentiality of the ledger and accounting documents which I work on, particularly the wages book, as I currently have nowhere to file these documents. When I am not in my office, including overnight, I have to leave the ledger and documents on my desk. This means potentially that anyone in the building, employees, customers, visitors etc could access the information contained in the documents.

I suggest that I have a lockable filing cabinet which I can use to store the ledger and documents safely when I am not working on them in my office.

45 CREDITORS' ACCOUNTS

Skelton Engineers
Smithson Ltd
Snipe Associates
Sonic Partners
Souter Finance
Spartan & Co

46 ACCOUNTS PERSONNEL

- Wages book - wages clerk
- Aged debtor analysis - sales ledger clerk
- Creditors' accounts - purchases ledger clerk
- Bank statement - cashier
- Petty cash book - petty cashier
- Credit limits for customers - sales ledger clerk
- Standing order schedule - cashier

Answers to practice devolved assessments

1: Comart Supplies Ltd

GENERAL LEDGER

Receipts - cash book

Date	Details	Discounts	Total received	VAT	Debtors	Other
		£	£	£	£	£
1 Jun	Silicon World	251	6,024		6,024	
1 Jun	Bristol Micros		7,687		7,687	
1 Jun	Sales		1,645	245		1,400
1 Jun	Silicon World		1,000		1,000	
			16,356	245	14,711	1,400
2 Jun	Balance b/d		8,046			

Payments - cash book

Date	Details	Discounts	Total paid	VAT	Creditors	Other
		£	£	£	£	£
1 Jun	Balance b/d		4,670			
1 Jun	ITC Computers	100	3,240		3,240	
1 Jun	Loan		400			400
1 Jun	Balance c/d		8,046			
			16,356		3,240	400

Bank loan

Date	Details	Amount	Date	Details	Amount
		£			£
1 Jun	Bank	400	1 Jun	Balance b/d	16,200
1 Jun	Balance c/d	15,800			
		16,200			16,200
			2 Jun	Balance b/d	15,800

Debtors control account

Date	Details	Amount	Date	Details	Amount
		£			£
1 Jun	Balance b/d	804,873	1 Jun	Sales returns	193
1 Jun	Sales	41,399	1 Jun	Bad debt	493
			1 Jun	Discount allowed	251
			1 Jun	Bank	6,024
			1 Jun	Bank	7,687
			1 Jun	Bank	1,000
			1 Jun	Balance c/d	830,624
		846,272			846,272
2 Jun	Balance b/d	830,624			

Answers to practice devolved assessments

Discount allowed

Date	Details	Amount	Date	Details	Amount
		£			£
1 Jun	Balance b/d	24,839			
1 Jun	Debtors control a/c	251	1 Jun	Balance c/d	25,090
		25,090			25,090
2 Jun	Balance b/d	25,090			

Discount received

Date	Details	Amount	Date	Details	Amount
		£			£
			1 Jun	Balance b/d	18,628
1 Jun	Balance c/d	18,728	1 Jun	Creditors control a/c	100
		18,728			18,728
			2 Jun	Balance b/d	18,728

Power and heating

Date	Details	Amount	Date	Details	Amount
		£			£
1 Jun	Balance b/d	487			
1 Jun	Creditors	626	1 Jun	Balance c/d	1,113
		1,113			1,113
2 Jun	Balance b/d	1,113			

Purchases

Date	Details	Amount	Date	Details	Amount
		£			£
1 Jun	Balance b/d	1,241,860			
1 Jun	Creditors	28,286	1 Jun	Balance c/d	1,270,146
		1,270,146			1,270,146
2 Jun	Balance b/d	1,270,146			

Sales

Date	Details	Amount	Date	Details	Amount
		£			£
			1 Jun	Balance b/d	1,655,960
			1 Jun	Debtors	35,234
1 Jun	Balance c/d	1,692,594	1 Jun	Bank	1,400
		1,692,594			1,692,594
			2 Jun	Balance b/d	1,692,594

VAT

Date	Details	Amount	Date	Details	Amount
		£			£
			1 Jun	Balance b/d	69,173
1 Jun	Purchases	5,143	1 Jun	Sales	6,165
1 Jun	Sales returns	29	1 Jun	Purchase returns	98
1 Jun	Balance c/d	70,509	1 Jun	Cash sales	245
		75,681			75,681
			2 Jun	Balance b/d	70,509

CREDITORS LEDGER

ITC Computers Ltd

Date	Details	Amount	Date	Details	Amount
		£			£
1 Jun	Purchase return	660	1 Jun	Balance b/d	25,689
1 Jun	Bank/Discount	3,340	1 Jun	Purchases	4,315
1 Jun	Balance c/d	26,004			
		30,004			30,004
			2 Jun	Balance b/d	26,004

2: Chang Fashions Ltd

GENERAL LEDGER

Creditors control account

Date	Details	Amount	Date	Details	Amount
		£			£
	Purchases returns	256	Nov 26	Balance c/d	177,774
	Bank £(7,420 + 1,204 + 12,143)	20,767		Purchases	55,236
	Discounts	160			
Dec 2	Balance c/d	211,827			
		233,010			233,010
			Dec 3	Balance b/d	211,827

Power and heating

Date	Details	Amount	Date	Details	Amount
		£			£
Nov 26	Balance b/d	7,122	Dec 2	Balance c/d	12,788
	Creditors	5,666			
		12,788			12,788
Dec 3	Balance b/d	12,788			

Purchases

Date	Details	Amount	Date	Details	Amount
		£			£
Nov 26	Balance b/d	1,066,213	Dec 2	Balance c/d	1,108,727
	Creditors	41,343			
	Bank £(1,376 – 205)	1,171			
		1,108,727			1,108,727
Dec 3	Balance b/d	1,108,727			

Sales returns

Date	Details	Amount	Date	Details	Amount
		£			£
Nov 26	Balance b/d	6,984	Dec 2	Balance c/d	7,218
	Bank £(275 – 41)	234			
		7,218			7,218
Dec 3	Balance b/d	7,218			

Answers to practice devolved assessments

Shop fittings

Date	Details	Amount	Date	Details	Amount
		£			£
Nov 26	Balance b/d	35,560	Dec 2	Balance c/d	36,956
	Bank £(1,640 – 244)	1,396			
		36,956			36,956
Dec 3	Balance b/d	36,956			

VAT

Date	Details	Amount	Date	Details	Amount
		£			£
	Purchases	8,227	Nov 26	Balance b/d	38,162
	Bank			Purchases returns	38
	Cash purchases	205		Sales	7,770
	Shop fittings	244			
	Repairs	13			
	Refunds	41			
Dec 2	Balance c/d	37,240			
		45,970			45,970
			Dec 3	Balance b/d	37,240

CREDITORS LEDGER

Southern Gas

Date	Details	Amount	Date	Details	Amount
		£			£
	Bank	1,204	Nov 26	Balance b/d	1,204
Dec 2	Balance c/d	3,108		Purchases	3,108
		4,312			4,312
			Dec 3	Balance b/d	3,108

Style Clothes Limited

Date	Details	Amount	Date	Details	Amount
		£			£
	Purchases returns	256	Nov 26	Balance b/d	32,417
	Bank	7,420		Purchases	9,736
	Discount	160			
Dec 2	Balance c/d	34,317			
		42,153			42,153
			Dec 3	Balance c/d	34,317

Answers to practice devolved assessments

UPDATED TRIAL BALANCE AT THE END OF THE WEEK

	Debit balances £	Credit balances £
Suppliers		
Style Clothes Ltd		34,317
South East Electric £(NIL + 3,550)		3,550
Southern Gas		3,108
Trend Imports Ltds £(45,862 + 17,907)		63,769
Other suppliers £(98,291 + 20,935 – 12,143)		107,083
Total		211,827
Other		
Bank		184
Purchases	1,108,727	
Sales £(1,453,420 +(52,170 – 7,770))		1,497,820
Purchases returns £(5,741 + 218)		5,959
Sales returns	7,218	
Power and heating	12,788	
Shop fittings	36,956	
Shop fittings repairs £(241 + 88 – 13)	316	
Bank interest received £(319 + 411)		730
VAT		37,240
Discount received £(4,337 + 160)		4,497
Other debit balances	1,542,632	
Other credit balances		950,380
Totals	2,708,637	2,708,637

3: MEL Motor Factors

General ledger

RECEIPTS: CASH BOOK

Date	Details	Discounts £	Total received £	VAT £	Debtors £	Other £
1 Jun	Balance b/f		4,120			
1 Jun	Bank interest		122			122
1 Jun	Motormania	78	1,472		1,472	
		78	5,714		1,472	122
	Balance b/f		1,324			

PAYMENTS: CASH BOOK

Date	Details	Discounts £	Total paid £	VAT £	Creditors £	Other £
1 Jun	Bank charges		210			210
1 Jun	Lombard Products Ltd	141	2,817		2,817	
1 Jun	Purchases		1,363	203		1,160
	Balance c/f		1,324			
		141	5,714	203	2,817	1,370

BANK CHARGES

Date	Details	Amount £	Date	Details	Amount £
1 Jun	Balance b/f	261			
1 Jun	Cash book	210	1 Jun	Balance c/f	471
		471			471
2 Jun	Balance b/f	471			

BANK INTEREST RECEIVED

Date	Details	Amount £	Date	Details	Amount £
			1 Jun	Balance b/f	103
1 Jun	Balance c/f	225	1 Jun	Cash book	122
		225			225
			2 Jun	Balance b/f	225

Answers to practice devolved assessments

DEBTORS CONTROL ACCOUNT

Date	Details	Amount £	Date	Details	Amount £
1 Jun	Balance b/f	720,643	1 Jun	Creditors control a/c	1,450
1 Jun	Sales	37,740	1 Jun	Cash book	1,472
			1 Jun	Discount allowed	78
			1 Jun	Sales	168
			1 Jun	Balance c/f	755,215
		758,383			758,383
2 Jun	Balance b/f	755,215			

DISCOUNT ALLOWED

Date	Details	Amount £	Date	Details	Amount £
1 Jun	Balance b/f	21,408			
1 Jun	Debtors control a/c	78	1 Jun	Balance c/f	21,486
		21,486			21,486
2 Jun	Balance b/f	21,486			

DISCOUNT RECEIVED

Date	Details	Amount £	Date	Details	Amount £
			1 Jun	Balance b/f	15,194
1 Jun	Balance c/f	15,335	1 Jun	Creditors control a/c	141
		15,335			15,335
			2 Jun	Balance b/f	15,335

PURCHASES

Date	Details	Amount £	Date	Details	Amount £
1 Jun	Balance b/f	2,652,194			
1 Jun	Bank	1,160			
1 Jun	Creditors	29,441	1 Jun	Balance c/f	2,682,795
		2,682,795			2,682,795
2 Jun	Balance b/f	2,682,795			

VAT

Date	Details	Amount £	Date	Details	Amount £
1 Jun	Creditors control account	5,153	1 Jun	Balance b/f	71,089
1 Jun	Debtors control account	25	1 Jun	Debtors control account	5,621
1 Jun	Cash	203			
1 Jun	Balance c/f	71,329			
		76,710			76,710
			2 Jun	Balance b/f	71,329

Answers to practice devolved assessments

Creditors ledger

LOMBARD PRODUCTS LTD

Date	Details	Amount £	Date	Details	Amount £
1 Jun	Cash book	2,817	1 Jun	Balance b/f	56,987
1 Jun	Discount	141	1 Jun	Purchases day book	7,727
1 Jun	Balance c/f	61,756			
		64,714			64,714
			2 Jun	Balance b/f	61,756

Debtors ledger

MOTORMANIA

Date	Details	Amount £	Date	Details	Amount £
1 Jun	Balance b/f	27,124	1 Jun	Sales returns	168
1 Jun	Sales day book	6,156	1 Jun	Bank	1,472
			1 Jun	Discount	78
			1 Jun	Balance c/f	31,562
		33,280			33,280
2 Jun	Balance b/f	31,562			

Answers to practice devolved assessments

4: Music World

General ledger

DEBTORS CONTROL ACCOUNT

20X3		£	20X3		£
1 Dec	Balance b/f	537,483	1 Dec	Sales returns	167
	Sales	24,587		Bank	1,755
	Bank	1,000		Discounts allowed	45
				Balance c/f	561,103
		563,070			563,070
2 Dec	Balance b/f	561,103			

CREDITORS CONTROL ACCOUNT

20X3		£	20X3		£
1 Dec	Purchases returns	32	1 Dec	Balance b/f	404,546
	Bank £(4,388 + 10,565)	14,953		Purchases	29,310
	Discounts received	112			
	Balance c/f	418,759			
		433,856			433,856
			2 Dec	Balance b/f	418,759

EQUIPMENT

20X3		£	20X3		£
1 Dec	Balance b/f	4,182	1 Dec	Balance c/f	5,008
	Bank £(970 – 144)	826			
		5,008			5,008
2 Dec	Balance b/f	5,008			

HEATING AND LIGHTING

20X3		£	20X3		£
1 Dec	Balance b/f	1,728	1 Dec	Balance c/f	2,244
	Purchases	516			
		2,244			2,244
2 Dec	Balance b/f	2,244			

PURCHASES

20X3		£	20X3		£
1 Dec	Balance b/f	2,432,679	1 Dec	Balance c/f	2,457,304
	Creditors	24,429			
	Bank £(230 – 34)	196			
		2,457,304			2,457,304
2 Dec	Balance b/f	2,457,304			

Answers to practice devolved assessments

VAT

20X3		£	20X3		£
1 Dec	Purchases	4,365	1 Dec	Balance b/f	63,217
	Sales returns	25		Sales	3,662
	Bank	193		Purchases returns	5
	Balance c/f	62,301			
		66,884			66,884
			2 Dec	Balance b/f	62,301

Debtors ledger

CLASSIC MUSIC

20X3		£	20X3		£
1 Dec	Balance b/f	16,742	1 Dec	Sales returns	167
	Sales	1,978		Bank	1,755
	Bank	1,000		Discount	45
				Balance c/f	17,753
		19,720			19,720
2 Dec	Balance b/f	17,753			

Creditors ledger

ATLANTIC IMPORTS

20X3		£	20X3		£
1 Dec	Purchases returns	32	1 Dec	Balance b/f	43,607
	Bank	4,388		Purchases	12,528
	Discount	112			
	Balance c/f	51,603			
		56,135			56,135
			2 Dec	Balance b/f	51,603

Answers to practice devolved assessments

Updated trial balance at the end of the day

	£	£
Customers		
Hit Records Ltd £(10,841 + 4,279)	15,120	
Smiths & Co £(18,198 + 6,023)	24,221	
Classic Music	17,753	
Other customers £(491,702 + 12,307)	504,009	
Suppliers		
HMI Ltd £(82,719 + 10,524)		93,243
Atlantic Imports Ltd		51,603
Southern Electric £(nil + 606)		606
Other suppliers £(278,220 + 5,652 – 10,565)		273,307
Purchases	2,457,304	
Sales £(3,284,782 + 20,925)		3,305,707
Sales returns £(10,973 + 142)	11,115	
Purchases returns £(9,817 + 27)		9,844
Heating and lighting	2,244	
Equipment	5,008	
Equipment repairs £(166 + (102 – 15))	253	
Bank charges £(82 + 67)	149	
VAT		62,301
Bank		1,075
Discount allowed £(11,420 + 45)	11,465	
Discount received £(8,516 + 112)		8,628
Other debit balances	1,368,815	
Other credit balances		611,142
Totals	4,417,456	4,417,456

Answers to trial run devolved assessments

ANSWERS TO TRIAL RUN DEVOLVED ASSESSMENT:

T S STATIONERY

DO NOT TURN THIS PAGE UNTIL YOU HAVE COMPLETED THE TRIAL RUN DEVOLVED ASSESSMENT

Answers to trial run devolved assessment

Task 1

MAIN LEDGER ACCOUNTS

CREDITORS CONTROL ACCOUNT

		£			£
31 Mar	PRDB	141	27 Mar	Opening balance	14,325
			31 Mar	PDB	846

PURCHASES ACCOUNT

		£			£
27 Mar	Opening balance	166,280	31 Mar	Balance c/d	167,000
31 Mar	PDB	720			
		167,000			167,000
1 Apr	Balance b/d	167,000			

PURCHASES RETURNS ACCOUNT

		£			£
31 Mar	Balance c/d	4,300	27 Mar	Opening balance	4,180
			31 Mar	PRDB	120
		4,300			4,300
			1 Apr	Balance b/d	4,300

VAT ACCOUNT

		£			£
31 Mar	PDB	126	27 Mar	Opening balance	1,405
31 Mar	Balance c/d	1,300	31 Mar	PRDB	21
		1,426			1,426
			1 Apr	Balance b/d	1,300

SUBSIDIARY LEDGER ACCOUNTS

F P PAPER

		£			£
			27 Mar	Opening balance	3,825
			31 Mar	PDB	188

GIFT PRODUCTS LTD

		£			£
31 Mar	PRDB	94	27 Mar	Opening balance	4,661
			31 Mar	PDB	235

HARPER BROS

		£			£
31 Mar	PRDB	47	27 Mar	Opening balance	3,702
			31 Mar	PDB	141

J S TRADERS

		£			£
			27 Mar	Opening balance	2,137
			31 Mar	PDB	282

Answers to trial run devolved assessment

Task 2

Main ledger

CREDITORS CONTROL ACCOUNT

			£				£
31 Mar	PRDB		141	27 Mar	Opening balance		14,325
31 Mar	Balance c/d		15,030	31 Mar	PDB		846
			15,171				15,171
				1 Apr	Balance b/d		15,030

Subsidiary ledger

F P PAPER

			£				£
31 Mar	Balance c/d		4,013	27 Mar	Opening balance		3,825
				31 Mar	PDB		188
			4,013				4,013
				1 Apr	Balance b/d		4,013

GIFT PRODUCTS LTD

			£				£
31 Mar	PRDB		94	27 Mar	Opening balance		4,661
31 Mar	Balance c/d		4,802	31 Mar	PDB		235
			4,896				4,896
				1 Apr	Balance b/d		4,802

HARPER BROS

			£				£
31 Mar	PRDB		47	27 Mar	Opening balance		3,702
31 Mar	Balance c/d		3,796	31 Mar	PDB		141
			3,843				3,843
				31 Mar	Balance b/d		3,796

J S TRADERS

			£				£
31 Mar	Balance c/d		2,419	27 Mar	Opening balance		2,137
				31 Mar	PDB		282
			2,419				2,419
				1 Apr	Balance b/d		2,419

Reconciliation of creditors control account balance with total of balances in the subsidiary ledger

	£
F P Paper	4,013
Gift Products Ltd	4,802
Harper Bros	3,796
J S Traders	2,419
Creditors control account balance	15,030

Answers to trial run devolved assessment

Task 3

Main ledger

DEBTORS CONTROL ACCOUNT

		£			£
31 Mar	Balance b/d	23,230	31 Mar	Journal 336	400
31 Mar	Journal 337	100	31 Mar	Balance c/d	22,930
		23,330			23,330
1 April	Balance b/d	22,930			

SALES ACCOUNT

		£			£
31 Mar	Balance b/d	255,910	31 Mar	Balance b/d	255,810
			31 Mar	Journal 337	100
		255,910			255,910
			1 April	Balance b/d	255,910

BAD DEBTS EXPENSE ACCOUNT

		£		£
31 Mar	Journal 336	400		

Subsidiary ledger

RETAIL ENTERPRISES

		£		£
31 Mar	Balance b/d	5,114		

C CUMMINGS

		£			£
31 Mar	Balance b/d	400	31 Mar	Bad debt w/o	400

PALMER LIMITED

		£		£
31 Mar	Balance b/d	6,248		

REAPER STORES

		£		£
31 Mar	Balance b/d	5,993		

KNIGHT RETAIL

		£		£
31 Mar	Balance b/d	5,575		

**Reconciliation of debtors control account balance
with the total of the balances in the subsidiary ledger for debtors**

	£
Retail enterprises	5,114
C Cummings	-
Palmer Ltd	6,248
Reapers Stores	5,993
Knight Retail	5,575
	22,930

Tasks 4, 5 and 6

CASH BOOK					
RECEIPTS			**PAYMENTS**		
Date	*Details*	*£*	*Date*	*Details*	*Cheque No*	*£*
1 Mar	Balance b/d	3,668	5 Mar	Harper Bros	002643	2,558
7 Mar	Palmer Ltd	2,557	12 Mar	Gift Products	002644	3,119
15 Mar	Retails Engineering	4,110	18 Mar	F P Paper	002645	2,553
20 Mar	Reapers Stores	4,782	24 Mar	J S Traders	002646	983
28 Mar	Knight Retail	3,765	31 Mar	BACS - wages		3,405
			31 Mar	SO rates		200
31 Mar	Bank interest	20	31 Mar	SO - loan		400
			31 Mar	Balance c/d		5,684
		18,902				18,902
1 April	Balance b/d	5,684				

RATES ACCOUNT

		£			£
31 Mar	Balance b/dB	2,200	31 Mar	Balance c/d	2,400
31 Mar	CBP	200			
		2,400			2,400
1 Apr	Balance b/d	2,400			

LOAN ACCOUNT

		£			£
31 Mar	CPB	400	31 Mar	Balance b/d	6,400
31 Mar	Balance c/d	6,000			
		6,400			6,400
			1 April	Balance b/d	6,000

BANK INTEREST RECEIVABLE

		£			£
			31 Mar	Balance b/d	100
31 Mar	Balance c/d	120	31 Mar	CRB	20
		120			120
			1 Apr	Balance b/d	120

Answers to trial run devolved assessment

Reasons why the cash book balance does not equal the bank statement balance:

- Cheque number 002646 for £983 is in the cash book but has not yet appeared on the bank statement.

- The receipt from Knight Retail for £3,765 is in the cash book but has not yet appeared on the bank statement.

Task 7

WAGES CONTROL ACCOUNT

		£			£
31 Mar	CPB - net wages	3,405	31 Mar	Wages expense	4,500
31 Mar	Inland revenue	720	31 Mar	Wages expense	420
31 Mar	Inland revenue	375			
31 Mar	Inland revenue	420			
		4,920			4,920

WAGES EXPENSE ACCOUNT

		£			£
1 Mar	Balance b/d	54,120			
31 Mar	Wages control	4,500			
31 Mar	Wages control	420	31 Mar	Balance c/d	59,040
		59,040			59,040
1 Apr	Balance b/d	59,040			

INLAND REVENUE ACCOUNT

		£			£
			31 Mar	Wages control	720
			31 Mar	Wages control	375
31 Mar	Balance c/d	1,515	31 Mar	Wages control	420
		1,515			1,515
			1 Apr	Balance b/d	1,515

Task 8

Voucher total

Voucher number	£
0264	3.67
0265	9.48
0266	6.70
0267	13.20
0268	2.36
0269	1.55
0270	10.46
0271	4.89
0272	3.69
	56.00

Cash

Note/coin	Number	£
£10	1	10.00
£5	4	20.00
£2	2	4.00
£1	7	7.00
50p	3	1.50
20p	4	0.80
10p	5	0.50
5p	1	0.05
2p	7	0.14
1p	1	0.01
		44.00

	£
Voucher total	56.00
Cash total	44.00
Imprest amount	100.00

The petty cash balance to appear in the trial balance is £44.00

Task 9

Product X2635

Stores records	125 units
Stock count	120 units

There are a number of possible reasons for the difference.

(a) An issue of five units has not been recorded in the stock records. However, given the size of the other issues this seems unlikely.

(b) Five units of stock were damaged and therefore were destroyed but this was not recorded in the stock records.

(c) An error was made when writing up the stock record - either a purchase was recorded at 5 units too large or an issue was recorded as 5 units too small.

(d) Five units of the product may have been stolen.

Product F3398

Stores records	25 units
Stock count	175 units

There are a number of possible reasons for the difference.

(a) Errors could have been made in writing up the stores records.

(b) As the purchases seem to be amounts of 150 units each time it seems most likely that a purchase has been made around the month end that has not yet been recorded in the stores records. If 150 units had been purchased then this would give a month end balance of 175 units.

Answers to trial run devolved assessment

Task 10

Trial balance at 31 March 20X1

	£	£
Building	100,000	
Motor vehicles	34,500	
Office equipment	13,000	
Purchases (Task 1)	167,000	
Purchases returns (Task 1)		4,300
Capital		160,000
Sales (Task 3)		255,910
Sales returns	6,800	
Discounts allowed	300	
Stock	16,000	
Loan (Task 6)		6,000
Discount received		600
Debtors (Task 3)	22,930	
Petty cash (Task 8)	44	
Creditors (Task 2)		15,030
VAT (Task 1)		1,300
Bank (Task 5)	5,684	
Inland revenue (Task 7)		1,515
Wages (Task 7)	59,040	
Motor expenses	4,297	
Telephone	4,850	
Electricity	3,630	
Rates (Task 6)	2,400	
Miscellaneous expenses	3,900	
Bad debts expense (Task 3)	400	
Bank interest receivable (Task 6)		120
	444,775	444,775

Task 11

MEMO

To: The owner
From: The bookkeeper
Date: 2 April 20X1
Subject: Errors and the trial balance

Although the trial balance does balance at the year end this does not necessarily mean that there are no errors in the accounting records. There are some types of errors that are not revealed by extracting a trial balance as they do not cause an imbalance on the trial balance. These types of errors are:

Error of omission - this is where an entry has not been made in the accounting records at all - therefore there has been neither a debit nor a credit entry. For example, if the journal entry for the bad debt write off had not been posted to the ledger accounts this would not have affected the balancing of the trial balance.

Error of commission - here the double entry has taken place but one side of the entry has been to the correct type of account but to the wrong account. For example, suppose payment of the telephone bill had been credited in the bank account but then debited to the electricity account. Both the telephone account and the electricity account are incorrect but the trial balance still balances.

Error of principle - here one side of the double entry has been to the wrong type of account. For example if the cost of petrol, a motor expense, had been debited to the motor vehicle fixed asset account the trial balance would still balance but the fixed asset account and the expense account for the motor vehicle would be incorrect.

Reversal of entries - here a debit and matching credit entry are made to the correct accounts but to the wrong side of each account. For example if the bad debt write off was accounted for as a debit to the debtors control account and a credit to the bad debts expense account this would not affect the balancing of the trial balance but both the debtors control account and bad debts expense account balances would be incorrect.

Error of original entry - with this type of error the correct accounts are debited and credited but with the incorrect amount. For example if the payment of the telephone bill of say £1,200 was entered in both the cash book and the telephone account as £2,100 the trial balance would still balance but the bank account and telephone account balances would be incorrect.

Compensating errors - this type of error is where two errors are made which exactly cancel each other out. For example if the bank interest receivable account balance was listed in the trial balance at £100 too large and the miscellaneous expenses account balance was also listed as £100 too large then the two errors would cancel each other out and the trial balance would still balance.

ANSWERS TO AAT SAMPLE SIMULATION

**DO NOT TURN THIS PAGE UNTIL YOU HAVE
COMPLETED THE AAT SAMPLE SIMULATION**

ANSWERS

Task 1

CREDITORS CONTROL ACCOUNT

Date 20X0	Details	Amount £	Date 20X0	Details	Amount £
31 Aug	Purchases returns	940	1 Aug	Balance b/f	33,600
31 Aug	Discounts received	100	31 Aug	Purchases	31,725
31 Aug	Bank	34,155			
31 Aug	Balance c/d	30,130			
		65,325			65,325
			1 Sept	Balance b/d	30,130

RECONCILIATION OF CREDITORS CONTROL ACCOUNT
WITH SUBSIDIARY (PURCHASES) LEDGER
AS AT 31 AUGUST 20X0

	£
Closing balance of creditors control account	30,130
Total balance of accounts in subsidiary (purchases) ledger	30,130
Imbalance	NIL

Task 2

BAD DEBTS WRITTEN OFF

Date 20X0	Details	Amount £	Date 20X0	Details	Amount £
31 August	Balance b/f	150	31 August	Balance c/d	750
31 August	JNL30	600			
		750			750
1 Sept	Balance b/d	750			

VAT

Date 20X0	Details	Amount £	Date 20X0	Details	Amount £
31 August	Purchases	4,725	1 August	Balance b/f	14,269
31 August	Sales credits	70	31 August	Purchase credits	140
31 August	JNL 30	105	31 August	Sales	6,125
31 August	Balance c/d	15,634			
		20,534			20,534
			1 Sept	Balance b/d	15,634

Answers to AAT sample simulation

SALES

Date 20X0	Details	Amount £	Date 20X0	Details	Amount £
31 August	JNL 31	1	1 August	Balance b/f	91,676
31 August	Balance c/d	132,800	31 August	Debtors	41,125
		132,801			132,801
			1 Sept	Balance b/d	132,800

Task 2 continued; Task 3

DEBTORS CONTROL ACCOUNT

Date 20X0	Details	Amount £	Date 20X0	Details	Amount £
1 August	Balance b/f	91,403	31 August	JNL 30	705
31 August	Sales	41,125	31 August	JNL 31	1
			31 August	Sales returns	470
			31 August	Discounts allowed	50
			31 August	Bank	36,824
			31 August	Balance c/d	94,478
		132,528			132,528
1 Sept	Balance b/d	94,478			

RECONCILIATION OF DEBTORS CONTROL ACCOUNT
WITH SUBIDIARY (SALES) LEDGER
AT 31 AUGUST 20X0

	£
Closing balance of debtors control account	94,479
Total balance of accounts in subsidiary (sales) ledger	94,030
Imbalance	448

NOTE TO CAROLYN

There is an imbalance between the debtors control account and subsidiary (sales) ledger of £448. This may be for any number of reasons, but the most likely explanation is that the account of Leasowes Ltd has a credit balance of £224. We may need to check whether this credit balance ought to be there. Whether the sales ledger or the control account is incorrect, the difference would be £224 × 2, ie £448.

Answers to AAT sample simulation

Task 4

TRIAL BALANCE AS AT 31 AUGUST 20X0

	Debit £	Credit £
Motor vehicle	21,500	
Office equipment	2,000	
Stock	34,800	
Bank	6,700	
Debtors control	94,478	
Creditors control		30,130
VAT		15,634
Capital		99,200
Loan from bank		2,200
Sales		132,800
Sales returns	1,175	
Purchases	94,876	
Purchases returns		200
Bank charges	50	
Discounts allowed	60	
Discounts received		160
Wages	18,346	
Rent and rates	1,080	
Electricity	800	
Telephone	756	
Motor expenses	2,470	
Bad debts written off	750	
Miscellaneous expenses		
Total	279,841	280,324

Note for Carolyn

The trial balance as at 31 August 20X0 has an imbalance of £483. This may have arisen because the figure for miscellaneous expenses has been omitted.

Task 5

Note for Carolyn

I feel I should draw your attention to the fact that the ledgers are kept on the top of my desk in reception. I am concerned that there may be a problem with confidentiality.

It would be a good idea to have a lockable filing cabinet so that I can lock the ledgers away when I am away from my desk or at night.

Tasks 6, 7, 8

CASH BOOK

Date 20X0	Details	Bank £	Date 20X0	Cheque number	Details	Bank £
1 Sept	Balance b/f	6,700	1 Sept	108300	J Green	600
1 Sept	L Townley	200	5 Sept	108301	Design Duo	235
28 Sept	Weston Wigg	1,200	25 Sept	108302	Carey Insurers	315
29 Sept	KKG Ltd	72	29 Sept	108303	Baxters Ltd	80
8 Sept	Centra Sales	2,000	15 Sept		Salaries	4,512
15 Sept	Bradford Ltd	1,000	26 Sept		East Council	150
			24 Sept		District Bank	200
					Bank charges	66
					Balance c/d	5,014
		11,172				11,172
1 Oct	Balance b/d	5,014				

Tasks 9

REASONS WHY THE CASH BOOK BALANCE DIFFERS FROM BANK STATEMENT

1. Receipt from Weston Wigg of £1,200 is recorded in the cash book but not on the bank statement.

2. Receipt from KKG Ltd of £72 is recorded in the cash book but not on the bank statements.

3. Payment to Carey Insurers of £315 is recorded in the cash book but not the bank statement.

Answers to AAT sample simulation

Task 10

MAIN (NOMINAL) LEDGER

DEBTORS CONTROL ACCOUNT

Date 20X0	Details	Amount £	Date 20X0	Details	Amount £
1 Sept	Balance b/f	94,478	1 Sept	L Townley	200
30 Sept	Sales	47,000	28 Sept	Weston Wigg	1,200
			29 Sept	KKG Ltd	72
			8 Sept	Centra Sales	2,000
			15 Sept	Bradford Ltd	1,000
			30 Sept	Balance c/d	137,006
		141,478			141,478
1 Oct	Balance b/d	137,006			

RENT AND RATES

Date 20X0	Details	Amount £	Date 20X0	Details	Amount £
1 Sept	Balance b/f	1,080	30 Sept	Balance c/d	1,230
15 Sept	Bank	150			
		1,230			1,230
1 Oct	Balance b/d	1,230			

LOAN

Date 20X0	Details	Amount £	Date 20X0	Details	Amount £
26 Sept	Bank	200	1 Sept	Balance b/f	2,200
30 Sept	Balance c/d	2,000			
		2,200			2,200
			1 Oct	Balance b/d	2,000

BANK CHARGES

Date 20X0	Details	Amount £	Date 20X0	Details	Amount £
1 Sept	Balance b/f	50	30 Sept	Balance c/d	116
24 Sept	Bank	66			
		116			116
1 Oct	Balance b/d	116			

PURCHASES

Date 20X0	Details	Amount £	Date 20X0	Details	Amount £
1 Sept	Balance b/f	94,876	30 Sept	Balance c/d	104,650
30 Sept	Creditors	9,774			
		104,650			104,650
1 Oct	Balance b/d	104,650			

VAT

Date 20X0	Details	Amount £	Date 20X0	Details	Amount £
30 Sept	Purchases	1,710	1 Sept	Balance b/f	15,634
30 Sept	Balance c/d	20,924	30 Sept	Sales	7,000
		22,634			22,634
			1 Oct	Balance b/d	20,924

CREDITORS CONTROL

Date 20X0	Details	Amount £	Date 20X0	Details	Amount £
1 Sept	J Green	600	1 Sept	Balance b/f	30,130
5 Sept	Design Duo	235	30 Sept	Purchases	11,484
25 Sept	Carey Insurers	315			
29 Sept	Baxters Ltd	80			
30 Sept	Balance c/d	40,384			
		41,614			41,614
			1 Oct	Balance b/d	40,384

Answers to AAT sample simulation

Task 11

COMPUTER SUMMARY
SALARIES FOR MONTH ENDED 20 SEPTEMBER 20X0

Employee	Gross pay £	Tax £	Employee's NIC £	Employer's NIC £	Net pay £
Carolyn Allday	2,000.00	389.00	167.00	199.00	1,444.00
Jennifer Stone	1,690.00	290.00	140.00	160.00	1,260.00
Barry Glazier	1,140.00	145.00	85.00	95.00	910.00
A Student	1,100.00	125.00	77.00	89.00	898.00
	5,930.00	949.00	469.00	543.00	4,512.00

WAGES CONTROL

Date 20X0	Details	Amount £	Date 20X0	Details	Amount £
30 Sept	Net pay PAYE Employees' NIC Employer's NIC	4,512 949 469 543 6,473	30 Sept	Gross wages Employer's NIC	5,930 543 6,473

Task 12

STORES RECORD CARD – V800 INDUSTRIAL VACUUM CLEANER

Date	Details	In	Out	Quantity in stock	@ £50 per vacuum £
1 Sept	Opening balance			174	8,700
1 Sept	Sales		10	164	8,200
4 Sept	Sales		20	144	7,200
6 Sept	Sales		50	94	4,700
7 Sept	Sales		15	79	3,950
11 Sept	Sales		20	59	2,950
12 Sept	Faulty		1	58	2,900
13 Sept	Sales		20	38	1,900
15 Sept	Sales		20	18	900
18 Sept	Receipt	100		118	5,900
20 Sept	Sales		10	108	5,400
22 Sept	Sales		5	103	5,150
25 Sept	Sales		15	88	4,400
26 Sept	Sales		20	68	3,400
28 Sept	Receipt	110		178	8,900
29 Sept	Sales		20	158	7,900
30 Sept	Sales		20	138	6,900

Answers to AAT sample simulation

RECONCILIATION OF STOCK RECORD WITH PHYSICAL STOCK CHECK ON 30 SEPTEMBER 20X0

PHYSICAL STOCK CHECK: 139 @ £50	£6,950
STORES RECORD CARD BALANCE	£6,900
DIFFERENCE	£50

Note for Carolyn – V800

There is a difference of £50 between the stock valuation per the physical stock check and the valuation calculated using the updated stores record card. This may be due to the faulty V800 on 12 Sept. This may have been included n the physical stock check, while it has been deducted from the stores record card.

Answers to AAT sample simulation

Task 13

TRIAL BALANCE AS AT 30 SEPTEMBER 20X0

	Debit £	Credit £
Motor vehicle	21,500	
Office equipment	2,000	
Stock	34,800	
Bank	5,014	
Debtors control	137,006	
Creditors control		40,384
Inland Revenue		1,961
VAT		20,924
Capital		99,200
Loan from bank		2,000
Sales		172,800
Sales returns	1,175	
Purchases	104,650	
Purchases returns		200
Bank charges	116	
Discounts allowed	60	
Discounts received		160
Wages	24,819	
Rent and rates	1,230	
Electricity	800	
Telephone	756	
Motor expenses	2,470	
Bad debts written off	750	
Miscellaneous expenses	483	
Total	**337,629**	**337,629**

Answers to AAT sample simulation

ASSESSMENT CRITERIA

Assessors must refer to the Standards of Competence for Accounting and be guided by the performance criteria when evaluating candidates' work.

PART 1

Task 1 (3.2 (i)(ii))

Candidates should make entries to the control account and show clearly the balance carried down, and identify that there is no imbalance.

One error is allowed in this section.

Task 2 (3.2 (i)(iii))

The journal entries should be accurately recorded in the relevant ledger accounts and three of the accounts totalled, with the balance carried down clearly labelled.

Two errors are allowed in this section.

Task 3 (3.2 (i)(ii)(iv))

Candidates should make the relevant entries in the debtors control account and clearly show the balance carried down. The reconciliation statement should identify the imbalance of £448. The note to Carolyn should ideally suggest that the credit balance in the subsidiary (sales) ledger of £224 may be the reason for the imbalance, although other plausible answers should be accepted.

Two errors are allowed in this section.

Task 4 (3.3 (i)(ii)(iii)(iv))

Candidates should be able to transfer the list of given balances to the trial balance and locate balances from elsewhere in the simulation to transfer.

The note to Carolyn should ideally suggest that there is a missing figure, namely miscellaneous expenses, but other plausible answers should be accepted.

Four errors are allowed in this section.

Task 5 (3.2 (v))

Candidates should recognise that the ledgers should be locked away in a filing cabinet when away from a work station.

PART 2

Task 6 (3.1 (i))

Candidates should update the cash book with two standing orders and two credit transfers and recognise that the standing order to Bakers Rentals has not yet commenced.

Tasks 7, 8 and 9 (3.1 (ii)(iii)(iv))

Candidates should carry out the matching process, update the cash book with bank charges and total the cash book with the balance carried down clearly labelled. Candidates should also recognise the three items which do not yet appear in the bank statement.

Two errors are allowed in this section.

Answers to AAT sample simulation

Task 10 (3.2 (i))

Accurate entries should be made into the appropriate ledger accounts and all accounts totalled, showing clearly the balances carried down.

Two errors are allowed in this section.

Task 11 (3.2 (ii))

Candidates should make accurate entries and total the wages control account.

No errors are allowed in this section.

Task 12 (3.2 (ii)(iv))

Candidates should accurately complete the calculations on the stores record card and identify the imbalance. The note to Carolyn should ideally identify the faulty item of stock but other plausible answers should be accepted.

Two errors are allowed in this section.

Task 13 (3.3 (i)(iii))

Candidates should be able to transfer the list of given balances to the trial balance and locate balances from elsewhere in the simulation to transfer.

Four errors are allowed in this section.

OVERALL ASSESSMENT

Candidates may be allowed to make further minor errors, provided such errors do not suggest a fundamental lack of understanding.

Candidates must not be penalised more than once for an error. If a candidate transfers an incorrect figure to another part of the exercise, this is not counted as a further error.

General

- It is expected that work will be neatly and competently presented.
- Pencil is not acceptable.
- Liquid correcting fluid may be used but it should be used in moderation.

Discretion

In having regard to the above criteria, the assessor is entitled in marginal cases to exercise discretion in the candidate's favour. Such discretion shall only be exercised where other criteria are met to above the required standard, and in the opinion of the assessor, the assessment overall demonstrates competence and would be an acceptable standard in the workplace.

Answers to trial run central assessments

ANSWERS TO TRIAL RUN CENTRAL ASSESSMENT 1

DO NOT TURN THIS PAGE UNTIL YOU HAVE COMPLETED TRIAL RUN CENTRAL ASSESSMENT 1

Answers to trial run central assessments

SECTION 1: PROCESSING EXERCISE

SALES LEDGER

Bijoux Ltd

Date	Details	Amount	Date	Details	Amount
		£			£
1 June	Balance b/d	11,715	1 June	Bank	11,515
	Sales day book	1,692		Discounts allowed	200
				Balance c/d	1,692
		13,407			13,407
2 June	Balance b/d	1,692			

Gee & Law Ltd

Date	Details	Amount	Date	Details	Amount
		£			£
1 June	Bank	100	1 June	Balance b/d	100

J Llewellyn & Sons Ltd

Date	Details	Amount	Date	Details	Amount
		£			£
1 June	Balance b/d	4,520	1 June	Sales returns day book	470
	Sales day book	1,880		Balance c/d	5,930
		6,400			6,400
2 June	Balance b/d	5,930			

H Stanton Plc

Date	Details	Amount	Date	Details	Amount
		£			£
1 June	Balance b/d	18,900	1 June	Sales returns day book	376
	Sales day book	6,768		Bank	8,260
	Sales day book	7,520		Balance c/d	24,552
		33,188			33,188
2 June	Balance b/d	24,552			

York Jewellers

Date	Details	Amount	Date	Details	Amount
		£			£
1 June	Balance b/d	6,300	1 June	Bank	3,136
	Sales day book	2,632		Discounts allowed	64
	Sales day book	940		Balance c/d	6,672
		9,872			9,872
2 June	Balance b/d	6,672			

GENERAL LEDGER

Sales Ledger Control

Date	Details	Amount	Date	Details	Amount
		£			£
1 June	Balance b/d	86,200	1 June	Sales returns day book	846
	Sales day book	21,432		Bank	22,911
	Bank	100		Discounts allowed	264
				Balance c/d	83,711
		107,732			107,732
2 June	Balance b/d	83,711			

Sales

Date	Details	Amount	Date	Details	Amount
		£			£
1 June	Balance c/d	998,240	1 June	Balance b/d	980,000
				Debtors	18,240
		998,240			998,240
			2 June	Balance b/d	998,240

Sales Returns

Date	Details	Amount	Date	Details	Amount
		£			£
1 June	Balance b/d	12,630		Balance c/d	13,350
	Debtors	720			
		13,350			13,350
2 June	Balance b/d	13,350			

Answers to trial run central assessments

Discounts allowed

Date	Details	Amount	Date	Details	Amount
		£			£
1 June	Balance b/d	13,100		Balance c/d	13,364
	Debtors	264			
		13,364			13,364
2 June	Balance b/d	13,364			

VAT

Date	Details	Amount	Date	Details	Amount
		£			£
1 June	Sales returns day book	126	1 June	Balance b/d	16,350
	Balance c/d	19,416		Sales day book	3,192
		19,542			19,542
			2 June	Balance b/d	19,416

JOURNAL

Date	Details	Debit	Credit
1 June	TPA Bullion plc sales ledger	7,050	
	TP Bullock plc sales ledger		7,050
1 June	Bank charges	118	
	Interest received		118
1 June	Fixed assets: machinery	400	
	VAT	70	
	Creditors (or Excel Machines Ltd)		470

UPDATED TRIAL BALANCE

	Debit balances	Credit balances
	£	£
Sales ledger control	83,711	
Sales		998,240
Sales returns	13,350	
Discounts allowed	13,364	
VAT		19,416
Other debit balances	1,416,059	
Other credit balances		508,828
Totals	1,526,484	1,526,484

Answers to trial run central assessments

SECTION 2: TASKS AND QUESTIONS

1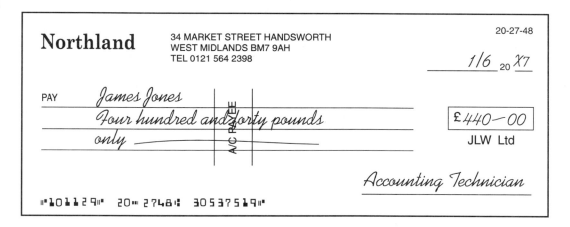

2 (a) A standing order (the recipient cannot change the amount).

   (b) A cheque written now but with a later date shown; in theory it cannot be honoured until that date.

3 (a) Yes
   (b) No
   (c) Yes

4 (a) DEBIT   Purchase control account   £235
       CREDIT   VAT   £35
       CREDIT   Purchases/purchases returns   £200

   (b) VAT = £2,600 × 98% × 17.5% = £445.90

   (c) Debited

5 (a) No

   (b) Banks will treat such multiple cheques as applying to only one transaction and so the credit limit of £100 applies to the combined total of the cheques.

6 A proforma invoice is used to obtain payment in advance of goods being sent, ie instead of being sent with or after the goods to request payment.

7 Bankers Automated Clearing System

8 (a) Visual display unit
   (b) Random access memory
   (c) Read only memory

Answers to trial run central assessments

9

Wages Control Account

Date 20X0	Details	Amount £	Date 20X0	Details	Amount £
30 June	Net pay	13,536	30 June	Gross wages	17,790
	PAYE	2,847		Employer's NIC	1,629
	Employees' NIC	1,407			
	Employer's NIC	1,629			
		19,419			19,419

10
- Calculation error in stock record
- Error in physical count of stock
- Error in stock receipt entry on stock record
- Damaged stock
- Theft

ANSWERS TO TRIAL RUN CENTRAL ASSESSMENT 2

DO NOT TURN THIS PAGE UNTIL YOU HAVE COMPLETED TRIAL RUN CENTRAL ASSESSMENT 2

Answers to trial run central assessments

SECTION 1: PROCESSING EXERCISE

SALES LEDGER

H Booth Limited

Date	Details	Amount	Date	Details	Amount
20X8		£	20X8		£
June 1	Balance b/d	8,225	June 1	Bank	2,350
June 1	Sales	1,692	June 1	Discounts Allowed	200
June 1	Sales	2,021	June 1	Balance c/d	9,388
		11,938			11,938
June 2	Balance b/d	9,388			

T Burbridge Limited

Date	Details	Amount	Date	Details	Amount
20X8		£	20X8		£
June 1	Balance b/d	7,050	June 1	Bank	940
June 1	Sales	470	June 1	Balance c/d	6,580
		7,520			7,520
June 2	Balance b/d	6,580			

The Peters Partnership

Date	Details	Amount	Date	Details	Amount
20X8		£	20X8		£
June 1	Balance b/d	5,875	June 1	Balance c/d	8,225
June 1	Sales	2,350			
		8,225			8,225
June 2	Balance b/d	8,225			

W Dalton Limited

Date	Details	Amount	Date	Details	Amount
20X8		£	20X8		£
June 1	Balance b/d	29,375	June 1	Bank	15,275
June 1	Sales	752	June 1	Balance c/d	14,946
June 1	Sales	94			
		30,221			30,221
June 2	Balance b/d	14,946			

GENERAL (MAIN) LEDGER

Sales

Date	Details	Amount	Date	Details	Amount
20X8		£	*20X8*		£
June 1	Balance c/d	732,786	June 1	Balance b/f	726,506
			June 1	Debtors	6,280
		732,786			732,786
			June 2	Balance b/d	732,786

Sales (Debtors) Ledger Control

Date	Details	Amount	Date	Details	Amount
20X8		£	*20X8*		£
June 1	Balance b/f	162,150	June 1	Bank	18,565
June 1	Sales	7,379	June 1	Discounts Allowed	200
			June 1	Balance c/d	150,764
		169,529			169,529
June 2	Balance b/d	150,764			

Bank Charges

Date	Details	Amount	Date	Details	Amount
20X8		£	*20X8*		£
June 1	Balance b/f	967	June 1	Balance c/d	1,075
June 1	Bank	108			
		1,075			1,075
June 1	Balance b/d	1,075			

Discounts Allowed

Date	Details	Amount	Date	Details	Amount
20X8		£	*20X8*		£
June 1	Balance b/f	370	June 1	Balance c/d	570
June 1	Debtors	200			
		570			570
June 2	Balance b/d	570			

Answers to trial run central assessments

VAT

Date	Details	Amount	Date	Details	Amount
20X8		£	20X8		£
June 1	Balance c/d	16,464	June 1	Balance b/d	15,365
			June 1	Sales	1,099
		16,464			16,464
			June 2	Balance b/d	16,464

Bank Loan

Date	Details	Amount	Date	Details	Amount
20X8		£	20X8		£
June 1	Bank	450	June 1	Balance b/d	15,300
June 1	Balance c/d	14,850			
		15,300			15,300
			June 2	Balance b/d	14,850

Motor Vehicles

Date	Details	Amount	Date	Details	Amount
20X8		£	20X8		£
June 1	Balance b/d	17,650	June 1	Balance c/d	32,150
June 1	Bank	14,500			
		32,150			32,150
June 2	Balance b/d	32,150			

Motor Insurance

Date	Details	Amount	Date	Details	Amount
20X8		£	20X8		£
June 1	Balance b/d	495	June 1	Balance c/d	812
June 1	Bank	317			
		812			812
June 2	Balance b/d	812			

JOURNAL

Date	Details	Debit	Credit
20X8		£	£
June 1	Electricity	717	
June 1	Office Equipment		717
June 1	Belton Stationers	470	
June 1	Belton & Byng Ltd		470

UPDATED TRIAL BALANCE

	Debit balances	Credit balances
	£	£
Sales		732,786
Sales (debtors) ledger control	150,764	
Bank charges	1,075	
Discount allowed	570	
VAT		16,464
Bank loan		14,850
Motor vehicles	32,150	
Motor insurance	812	
Other debit balances	588,964	
Other credit balances		10,235
Totals	774,335	774,335

SECTION 2: TASKS AND QUESTIONS

1

PETTY CASH CONTROL

Date 20X1	Details	£	Date 20X1	Details	£
1 Jan	Balance b/f	350	31 Jan	Petty cash	250
31 Jan	Bank	300	31 Jan	Balance c/d	400
		650			650
1 Feb	Balance b/d	400			

2 (a)

			£	£
Debit	Bad debt expense (352.50 × 100/117.5)		300.00	
Debit	VAT		52.50	
Credit	Sales (debtors) ledger control			352.50

(b) Bad debts are an expense to the business which reduce profit. Also, since debtors are an asset, a bad debt write off results in a reduction in the assets of the business.

(c) (i) Delivery Note — This details the goods supplied and is sent with the goods to the purchaser.

(ii) Goods Received Note — This is an internal document used to record quantities and types of goods received into the purchaser's warehouse.

(iii) Advice Note — This is notification sent to the purchaser that goods have been dispatched.

3 This is the account of an individual or company in which details of their transactions would be recorded. For example a supplier account in the purchases ledger or a customer account in the sales ledger.

4 Any three of the following:

(a) Unrecorded lodgements (deposits).
(b) Unpresented cheques.
(c) Dishonoured cheques.
(d) Bank errors.
(e) Direct debits/standing orders.
(f) Bank charges/interest received.
(g) Cash book errors.

5 The drawer's bank is refusing to honour the cheque, usually because of insufficient funds.

6 (a) Capital.

(b) Training is usually classified as revenue expenditure, but the substantial nature of the training costs may mean that they are capitalised.

(c) Revenue.

Answers to trial run central assessments

7 Any two of the following:

(a) Computerised systems are more accurate.
(b) Data can be categorised/analysed more effectively.
(c) Large volumes of data can be processed quickly.
(d) Data is stored more securely.
(e) Data storage takes up less space.
(f) Computerised systems can be used by non-specialists.
(g) Data retrieval is easier.

8 (a) General (main) ledger
(b) General (main) ledger
(c) Purchases ledger

9 Any two of the following:

(a) Access to petty cash could be limited.

(b) A formal system could be adopted to monitor petty cash eg. an imprest system.

(c) Petty cash could be kept in a lockable tin.

(d) Petty cash could be kept in a secure place such as a lockable cupboard or drawer.

10
- Calculation error in stock record
- Error in physical count of stock
- Error in stock receipt entry on stock record
- Damaged stock
- Theft

ANSWERS TO AAT SPECIMEN CENTRAL ASSESSMENT

DO NOT TURN THIS PAGE UNTIL YOU HAVE
COMPLETED THE AAT SPECIMEN CENTRAL ASSESSMENT

SECTION 1

Tasks 1.1, 1.2 and 1.3

SUBSIDIARY (SALES) LEDGER

HTP Limited

Date 20X0	Details	Amount £	Date 20X0	Details	Amount £
31 May	Balance b/d	8,300	31 May	Sales returns	235
31 May	Sales	1,175	31 May	Balance c/d	9,240
		9,475			9,475
1 June	B/d	9,240			

B Avery & Company

Date 20X0	Details	Amount £	Date 20X0	Details	Amount £
31 May	Balance b/d	4,400	31 May	Bank	3,900
31 May	Sales	1,880	31 May	Discount allowed	100
			31 May	Balance c/d	2,280
		6,280			6,280
1 June	Balance b/d	2,280			

Garners Limited

Date 20X0	Details	Amount £	Date 20X0	Details	Amount £
31 May	Balance b/d	1,850	31 May	Balance c/d	3,495
31 May	Sales	1,645			
		3,495			3,495
1 June	Balance b/d	3,495			

Rowley & Rudge

Date 20X0	Details	Amount £	Date 20X0	Details	Amount £
31 May	Balance b/d	4,700	31 May	Sales returns	141
31 May	Sales	2,350	31 May	Bank	1,000
			31 May	Balance c/d	5,909
		7,050			7,050
1 June	Balance b/d	5,909			

MAIN (GENERAL) LEDGER

Sales

Date 20X0	Details	Amount £	Date 20X0	Details	Amount £
31 May	Balance c/d	231,185	31 May	Balance b/d	225,185
			31 May	Debtors	6,000
		231,185			231,185
			1 June	Balance b/d	231,185

Sales returns

Date 20X0	Details	Amount £	Date 20X0	Details	Amount £
31 May	Balance b/d	1,080	31 May	Balance c/d	1,400
31 May	Debtors	320			
		1,400			1,400
1 June	Balance b/d	1,400			

Debtors control

Date 20X0	Details	Amount £	Date 20X0	Details	Amount £
31 May	Balance b/d	63,816	31 May	Sales returns	376
31 May	Sales	7,050	31 May	Bank	4,900
			31 May	Discount allowed	100
			31 Nay	Balance c/d	65,490
		70,866			70,866
1 June	Balance b/d	65,490			

Bank charges

Date 20X0	Details	Amount £	Date 20X0	Details	Amount £
31 May	Balance b/d	100	31 May	Balance c/d	256
31 May	Bank	156			
		256			256
1 June	Balance b/d	256			

Discounts allowed

Date 20X0	Details	Amount £	Date 20X0	Details	Amount £
31 May	Balance b/d	700	31 May	Balance c/d	800
31 May	Debtors	100			
		800			800
1 June	Balance b/d	800			

Answers to AAT specimen central assessment

Motor tax and insurance

Date 20X0	Details	Amount £	Date 20X0	Details	Amount £
31 May	Balance b/d	180	31 May	Balance c/d	270
31 May	Bank	90			
		270			270
1 June	Balance b/d	270			

Charitable donations

Date 20X0	Details	Amount £	Date 20X0	Details	Amount £
31 May	Bank	50	31 May	Balance c/d	50
		50			50
1 June	Balance b/d	50			

VAT

Date 20X0	Details	Amount £	Date 20X0	Details	Amount £
31 May	Sales returns	56	31 May	Balance b/d	11,198
31 May	Balance c/d	12,192	31 May	Sales	1,050
		12,248			12,248
			1 June	Balance b/d	12,192

TRIAL BALANCE AS AT 31 MAY 20X0

	Debit £	Credit £
Motor vehicle	28,300	
Office equipment	7,000	
Stock	35,587	
Bank	8,204	
Cash	75	
Debtors control	65,490	
Creditors control		34,880
VAT		12,192
Capital		16,723
Sales		231,185
Sales returns	1,400	
Purchases	101,857	
Purchases returns		366
Bank charges	256	
Discounts allowed	800	
Discounts received		132
Wages	37,843	
Rent and rates	4,000	
Electricity	814	
Telephone	922	
Motor tax and insurance	270	
Motor fuel	780	
Charitable donations	50	
Miscellaneous expenses	1,830	
Total	295,478	295,478

Answers to AAT specimen central assessment

SECTION 2

2.1

<table>
<tr><th colspan="2">Midland Bank plc
Date 31.05.X0</th><th colspan="2">Date 31.05.X0
Cashier's stamp</th><th colspan="2">bank giro credit
Midland Bank plc
HALESOWEN
Account
PAPERSTOP
BUSINESS ACCOUNT
Paid in by/Ref A. Student
40-23-08 31176786 78</th><th colspan="2"></th></tr>
<tr><td>£50 Notes</td><td></td><td></td><td></td><td></td><td></td><td>£50 Notes</td><td></td></tr>
<tr><td>£20 Notes</td><td>20 00</td><td></td><td></td><td></td><td></td><td>£20 Notes</td><td>20 00</td></tr>
<tr><td>£10 Notes</td><td>30 00</td><td></td><td></td><td></td><td></td><td>£10 Notes</td><td>30 00</td></tr>
<tr><td>£5 Notes</td><td>15 00</td><td></td><td></td><td></td><td></td><td>£5 Notes</td><td>15 00</td></tr>
<tr><td>£2</td><td></td><td></td><td></td><td></td><td></td><td>£2</td><td></td></tr>
<tr><td>£1</td><td>4 00</td><td></td><td></td><td></td><td></td><td>£1</td><td>4 00</td></tr>
<tr><td>50p</td><td>2 00</td><td></td><td></td><td></td><td></td><td>50p</td><td>2 00</td></tr>
<tr><td>20p</td><td>2 00</td><td></td><td></td><td></td><td></td><td>20p</td><td>2 00</td></tr>
<tr><td>10p, 5p</td><td>1 20</td><td></td><td></td><td></td><td></td><td>10p, 5p</td><td>1 20</td></tr>
<tr><td>2p, 1p</td><td>80</td><td></td><td></td><td></td><td></td><td>2p, 1p</td><td>80</td></tr>
<tr><td>Total cash</td><td>75 00</td><td></td><td></td><td></td><td></td><td>Total cash</td><td>75 00</td></tr>
<tr><td>Cheques, PO's see over £</td><td>75 00</td><td></td><td></td><td></td><td></td><td>Cheques, Po's £</td><td>75 00</td></tr>
</table>

2.2 Printed brochures
Office stationery
Office equipment

2.3 Capital expenditure — Motor vehicle
New computer
Office equipment for use by Paperstop
Fixtures and fittings

Revenue expenditure — Telephone
Wages
Insurance
Stationery for use by Paperstop

Note. Other relevant answers will be accepted.

2.4 Any four from:

- Gross pay
- Net pay
- Employees' NIC
- Employers' NIC
- PAYE
- Pension contributions - employee
- Pension contributions - employer
- Charitable donations
- Trade Union fees

Note. Other relevant answers will be accepted.

2.5 (a) Order acknowledgement/confirmation
(b) Advice note
(c) Pro forma invoice
(d) Goods received note

2.6 Alphabetical

2.7

31 May 20X0	DEBIT	Bank charges paid	£100.00	
	CREDIT	Bank interest received		£100.00
31 May 20X0	DEBIT	Motor fuel account	£9.00	
	CREDIT	Bank		£9.00
31 May 20X0	DEBIT	Bad debts written off	£600.00	
	DEBIT	VAT	£105.00	
	CREDIT	Subsidiary (sales) ledger control		£705.00
	CREDIT	Gee & Company		£705.00

2.8 CREDITORS CONTROL ACCOUNT CHECK AS AT 31 MAY 20X0

	£	£
Balance as at 1 May 20X0		37,612
Purchase invoices received	5,413	
Purchase credit notes received	(874)	
Payments made	(6,981)	
Discounts received	(290)	
		(2,732)
Balance as at 31 May 20X0		34,880

2.9 Any two of the following.

(a) To check the accuracy of the entries made in the personal accounts

(b) To trace errors

(c) To provide an internal check. The person posting entries to the creditors control account will act as a check on a different person whose job it is to post entries to the purchase ledger accounts

(d) To provide a creditors balance quickly, eg for a trial balance

2.10 (a) CASH BOOK

Date 20X0	Details	Amount £	Date 20X0	Details	Amount £
1 May	Balance b/f	1,181	1 May	Downing & Co	100
1 May	B King	480	5 May	GPT Ltd	235
24 May	C West	8,000	12 May	H&L Insurers	6,821
25 May	L Kingsley	1,175	23 May	Conners Ltd	80
8 May	Bakers Ltd - BGC	3,000	16 May	Keen & Company D/D	850
			24 May	Bank charges	56
			25 May	Cox Cleaning D/D	150
			30 May	Balance c/d	5,544
		13,836			13,836

(b) Receipt of £1,175 from L Kingsley not on statement
Receipt of £8,000 from C West not on statement
Payment of £6,821 to H&L Insurers not on statement

ANSWERS TO DECEMBER 2000 CENTRAL ASSESSMENT

**DO NOT TURN THIS PAGE UNTIL YOU HAVE
COMPLETED THE DECEMBER 2000 CENTRAL ASSESSMENT**

SECTION 1

Tasks 1.1, 1,2 and 1.3

SUBSIDIARY (SALES) LEDGER

Cooks Company

Date 20X0	Details	Amount £	Date 20X0	Details	Amount £
30 Nov	Balance b/f	10,575	30 Nov	Bank	1,950
30 Nov	Sales	2,115	30 Nov	Discount allowed	50
			30 Nov	Balance c/d	10,690
		12,690			12,690
1 Dec	Balance b/d	10,690			

Bakers Dozen

Date 20X0	Details	Amount £	Date 20X0	Details	Amount £
30 Nov	Balance b/f	5,875	30 Nov	Sales returns	470
30 Nov	Sales	940	30 Nov	Balance c/d	6,345
		6,815			6,815
1 Dec	Balance b/d	6,345			

Pastry Case Limited

Date 20X0	Details	Amount £	Date 20X0	Details	Amount £
30 Nov	Balance b/f	11,750	30 Nov	Sales returns	1,175
30 Nov	Sales	8,225	30 Nov	Balance c/d	18,800
		19,975			19,975
1 Dec	Balance b/d	18,800			

Greenwoods Pies

Date 20X0	Details	Amount £	Date 20X0	Details	Amount £
30 Nov	Balance b/f	1,250	30 Nov	Bank	750
30 Nov	Sales	705	30 Nov	Balance c/d	1,205
		1,955			1,955
1 Dec	Balance b/d	1,205			

MAIN (GENERAL) LEDGER

Sales

Date 20X0	Details	Amount £	Date 20X0	Details	Amount £
30 Nov	Balance c/d	319,200	30 Nov	Balance b/f	309,000
			30 Nov	Debtors	10,200
		319,200			319,200
			1 Dec	Balance b/d	319,200

Sales returns

Date 20X0	Details	Amount £	Date 20X0	Details	Amount £
30 Nov	Balance b/f	2,968	30 Nov	Balance c/d	4,368
30 Nov	Debtors	1,400			
		4,368			4,368
1 Dec	Balance b/d	4,368			

Debtors control

Date 20X0	Details	Amount £	Date 20X0	Details	Amount £
30 Nov	Balance b/f	106,840	30 Nov	Sales returns	1,645
30 Nov	Sales	11,985	30 Nov	Bank	2,700
			30 Nov	Discount allowed	50
			30 Nov	Balance c/d	114,430
		118,825			118,825
1 Dec	Balance b/d	114,430			

Bank charges

Date 20X0	Details	Amount £	Date 20X0	Details	Amount £
30 Nov	Balance b/f	367	30 Nov	Balance c/d	454
30 Nov	Bank	87			
		454			454
1 Dec	Balance b/d	454			

Discounts allowed

Date 20X0	Details	Amount £	Date 20X0	Details	Amount £
30 Nov	Balance b/f	170	30 Nov	Balance c/d	220
30 Nov	Debtors	50			
		220			220
1 Dec	Balance b/d	220			

Insurance

Date 20X0	Details	Amount £	Date 20X0	Details	Amount £
30 Nov	Balance b/f	600	30 Nov	Balance c/d	1,300
30 Nov	Bank	700			
		1,300			1,300
1 Dec	Balance b/d	1,300			

Rent paid

Date 20X0	Details	Amount £	Date 20X0	Details	Amount £
30 Nov	Balance b/f	850	30 Nov	Balance c/d	1,150
30 Nov	Bank	300			
		1,150			1,150
1 Dec	Balance b/d	1,150			

VAT

Date 20X0	Details	Amount £	Date 20X0	Details	Amount £
30 Nov	Sales returns	245	30 Nov	Balance b/f	16,512
30 Nov	Balance c/d	18,052	30 Nov	Sales	1,785
		18,297			18,297
			1 Dec	Balance b/d	18,052

Tasks 1.4 and 1.5

Trial Balance as at 30 November 20X0

	Debit balances £	Credit balances £
Motor vehicles	37,200	
Office equipment	9,700	
Stock	56,540	
Bank	4,313	
Cash	190	
Debtors control	114,430	
Creditors control		47,910
VAT		18,052
Capital		19,381
Sales		319,200
Sales returns	4,368	
Purchases	126,003	
Purchases returns		459
Commissions paid	890	
Bank charges	454	
Discounts allowed	220	
Wages	42,078	
Insurance	1,300	
Rent paid	1,150	
Rates	1,200	
Electricity	981	
Telephone	1,585	
Motor expenses	900	
Miscellaneous expenses	1,500	
Totals	405,002	405,002

Answers to December 2000 central assessment

SECTION 2

Task 2.1

(a) (i) The cheque is not signed.
 (ii) The cheque is out of date.
 (iii) Words and figures differ.

(b) Write to the customer pointing out the error and returning the cheque. You would also ask the customer to issue a replacement.

Task 2.2

(a) Any *three* from:

 (i) Space saving
 (ii) Speed of processing
 (iii) Accuracy of processing
 (iv) Security
 (v) Ease of access
 (vi) Frees staff up for more interesting work

(b) Any *one* from:

 (i) Personnel
 (ii) Payroll
 (iii) Workers' time recording

Other relevant answers will be accepted.

Task 2.3

(a) It confirms that the total of the debit balances agrees with the total of the credit balances, thus testing that the double entry is correct.

(b) Final accounts may be easily prepared.

(c) All account balances can be seen at a glance.

Task 2.4

(a) Paying-in slip counterfoil
(b) Standing order schedule
(c) Bank statement

Task 2.5

(a) Statement
(b) Credit note
(c) Delivery note
(d) Advice note

Task 2.6

(a) (i) To ensure security of cash and cheques
 (ii) To comply with company policy/insurance regulations
 (iii) To ensure the bank balance is topped up for paying creditors

(b) Night safe facilities.

Other relevant answers will be accepted.

Answers to December 2000 central assessment

Task 2.7

(a) Keep important documents out of view when other people are in the office.
(b) Make sure that only authorised people are given confidential information.
(c) Shred documents when no longer needed.
(d) Lock filing cabinets and office doors when out of the office.

Other relevant answers will be accepted.

Task 2.8

			£	£
(a)	DEBIT	Rates	90	
	CREDIT	Rent paid		90
(b)	DEBIT	Commission paid	27	
	CREDIT	Bank		27
(c)	DEBIT	Bad debts	800	
	DEBIT	VAT	140	
	CREDIT	Debtors control		940

Task 2.9

(a)

Creditors control

Date 20X0	Details	Amount £	Date 20X0	Details	Amount £
30 Nov	Bank	2,833	30 Nov	Balance b/f	40,103
30 Nov	Discounts received	406	30 Nov	Purchases	11,750
30 Nov	Purchases returns	704			
30 Nov	Balance c/d	47,910			
		51,853			51,853
			1 Dec	Balance b/d	47,910

(b)

	£
Creditors control account balance as at 30 November 20X0	47,910
Total of subsidiary (purchases) ledger accounts as at 30 November 20X0	47,710
Difference	200

(c) It is possible that the £100 debit balance on the account of Condor Ltd should be a credit balance and that an error has been made in the posting.

Answers to December 2000 central assessment

Task 2.10

(a)

CASH BOOK

Date 20X0	Details	Amount £	Date 20X0	Cheque no.	Details	Amount £
1 Nov	Balance b/f	2,626	1 Nov	218465	Byng & Co	58
1 Nov	L Weston	580	5 Nov	218466	LTF Ltd	470
24 Nov	B Carter	2,350	12 Nov	218467	P & S Insurance	8,000
25 Nov	C Keats	7,990	23 Nov	218468	Derby & White	540
8 Nov	Creamy Cakes	6,600	29 Nov	218469	The Flour Mill	705
			16 Nov		BA Roberts Ltd	1,400
			24 Nov		Bank charges	108
			25 Nov		Land security	200
			30 Nov		Balance c/d	8,665
		20,146				20,146
1 Dec	Balance b/d	8,665				

(b) Receipt of £2,350 from B Carter is not on the statement.
Receipt of £7,990 from C Keats is not on the statement.
Payment of £470 to LTF Ltd is not on the statement.
Payment of £705 to The Flour Mill is not on the statement.

> **Tutorial note.** We can prove this is correct as follows.
>
> | | £ |
> |---|---|
> | Balance per bank statement | (500) |
> | Deduct unpresented cheques: £470 + £705 | (1,175) |
> | Add uncleared deposits: £2,350 + £7,990 | 10,340 |
> | Balance per cash book | 8,665 |

Lecturers' resource pack activities

Lecturers' practice activities

Lecturers' practice activities

CHAPTER 1: REVISION OF BASIC BOOKKEEPING

1 REVENUE   Pre-assessment

If revenue expenditure is treated as capital expenditure, then:

(a) the total of the expenses for the period will be:

Too high/Too low/Unaffected

(b) the value of the fixed assets will be:

Too high/Too how/Unaffected

2 CLASSIFY   Pre-assessment

Classify the following ledger accounts according to whether they represent asset, liability, expense or revenue.

(a) Stock

Asset / Liability / Expense / Revenue

(b) Rent received

Asset / Liability / Expense / Revenue

(c) Heat, light and water

Asset / Liability / Expense / Revenue

(d) Bank overdraft

Asset / Liability / Expense / Revenue

3 APPROPRIATE   Assessment

What would be the appropriate document to be used in each of the following cases?

(a) MEL Motor Factors Ltd sends out a document to a credit customer on a monthly basis summarising the transactions that have taken place and showing the amount owed by the customer.

(b) MEL Motor Factors Ltd sends out a document to a credit customer in order to correct an error where the customer has been overcharged on an invoice.

(c) MEL Motor Factors Ltd wishes to buy certain goods from a supplier and sends a document requesting that those goods should be supplied.

CHAPTER 2: RECORDING, SUMMARISING AND POSTING TRANSACTIONS

4   IMPREST   **Assessment**

The company operates its petty cash using the imprest system. The imprest amount is £250.00. At the end of a particular period the five analysis columns were totalled to give the following amounts.

Column 1	£26.19
Column 2	£45.27
Column 3	£6.94
Column 4	£12.81
Column 5	£14.38

How much cash would be required to restore the imprest amount for the following period?

£........................

5   PRIMARY RECORDS   **Pre-assessment**

The sales and purchases day books are primary records used for listing data taken from source documents. Double entry is carried out by transferring relevant totals from the day books into the general ledger.

True / False

CHAPTER 3: FROM LEDGER ACCOUNTS TO INITIAL TRIAL BALANCE

6 ADVANTAGES — Pre-assessment

Give two advantages of using a computerised accounting system.

....

....

7 MANUFACTURER — Assessment

A manufacturer sells a product to a wholesaler for £200 plus VAT of £35. The wholesaler sells the same product to a retailer for £280 plus VAT of £49. The retailer then sells the product to a customer for £320 plus VAT of £56. What is the total amount of VAT collectable by HM Customs & Excise relating to the product?

£........................

8 CHILDREN'S CLOTHES — Pre-assessment

Chang Fashions Ltd has recently purchased £10,000 of children's clothes (zero rated supplies). How much VAT will be collected from the sale of these clothes?

CHAPTER 4: BANK RECONCILIATIONS

9   DEBIT OR CREDIT   Pre-assessment

The following bank statement was received from the company's bankers on 2 June 20X3.

Midwest Bank plc

Future Electrical Ltd

Statement of Account

Account No 60413658   Statement Date: 1 June 20X3

Date	Details	Debit £	Credit £	Balance £
1 June	Balance forward			1,791
1 June	Dividend		104	1,895
1 June	Counter credit		7,084	8,979
1 June	GR Insurance DD	89		8,890
1 June	000415	300		8,590

In updating the cash book balance of £4,892:

(a) Which item or items should now be debited to the cash book?

£104/£7,084/£89/£300

(b) Which items or items should now be credited to the cash book?

£104/£7,084/£89/£300

10   FILL IN   Assessment

MMS Textiles Ltd banks at the Moxley branch of the Norwest Bank, sort code no 36-24-41, and its account number is 479836806.

Fill in the paying-in slip and counterfoil given below to bank the cash takings on 1 December which are as follows.

Four	£50 notes
Twenty-three	£20 notes
Thirty-two	£10 notes
Seven	£5 notes
Eight	50 pence coins
Twelve	10 pence coins

Lecturers' practice activities

11 NOT ACCEPTED Assessment

Midwest Bank Plc 101-103 Lower High Street, West Bromwich B72 3AZ 20-14-37

28 November 20X6

PAY Centro Steelstock Limited

One thousand four hundred and ten pounds

£ 1,401.00

MTL Limited

002719 201437 85930617

Give *two* reasons why the above cheque, received from a debtor, would not be accepted for payment if it was presented to Midwest Bank plc.

(a) ....

(b) ....

CHAPTER 5: STOCK AND BAD DEBTS

12 BANKRUPT *Assessment*

One of the company's customers has been declared bankrupt with little probability of paying his debt to the company of £147. The outstanding amount is to be written off as a bad debt.

(a) In which record of original entry would the write-off be entered?

(b) Which general ledger account would be debited and which credited in this respect?

Account debited *Account credited*

_____ _____

13 STOCK CONTROL *Pre-assessment*

What is a stock control account used for?

CHAPTER 6: DEBTORS CONTROL ACCOUNT

14 REASONS — Pre-assessment

Give two reasons for maintaining the debtors control account.

15 CONTRA — Pre-assessment

What double entry would you make in the general (main) ledger in respect of the following.

(a) A set off of £20 is to be made between Tompkinson & Co's accounts in the sales ledger and in the purchases ledger.

Debit   Amount   Credit   Amount

(b) The account of D L Mason who owes £1,214 is to be written off as a bad debt.

Debit   Amount   Credit   Amount

CHAPTER 7: CREDITORS CONTROL ACCOUNT — Pre-assessment

16　FILE, RECORD OR FIELD

In a computerised accounting system:

(a) The purchases ledger will be a:

File / Record / Field

(b) The amount owed to a particular supplier will be a:

File / Record / Field

(c) The account details of a particular supplier will be a:

File / Record / Field

17　ONE REASON — Pre-assessment

Give one reason for maintaining a creditors control account.

Lecturers' practice activities

CHAPTER 8: FILING

18 CODES — Pre-assessment

The cheque numbers in a cheque book are an example of:

A sequential code / a hierarchical code

19 METHODS — Pre-assessment

List two classification methods for filing documents and files.

(a) ....

(b) ....

20 DOCUMENTS — Assessment

Suggest one classification method of filing each of the following documents. Your answer should suggest a different classification method for each document.

(a) General corresponding
(b) Invoices
(c) Insurance policies

Lecturers' practice devolved assessments

Lecturers' practice devolved assessment
1 Future electrical

Performance criteria

The following performance criteria are covered in this Devolved Assessment.

Element 3.2 Prepare ledger balances and control accounts

1. Relevant accounts are totalled
2. Control accounts are reconciled with the totals of the balance in the subsidiary ledger where appropriate
3. Authorised adjustments are correctly processed and documented

Notes on completing the Assessment

This Assessment is designed to test your ability to post transactions correctly to the ledgers and reconcile control accounts.

You are allowed 2 hours to complete your work.

A high level of accuracy is required. Check your work carefully.

Correcting fluid may be used but should be used in moderation. Errors should be crossed out neatly and clearly. You should write in black ink and not in pencil.

A full answer to this Assessment is provided in the Lecturers' Resource Pack for Unit 3.

Future Electrical

The tasks in this processing exercise are based on the transactions of Future Electrical Ltd. This company, based in the UK, buys and sells goods mainly on credit terms. The premises in Banbury consist of a warehouse, offices and a showroom with sales area used to sell goods directly to the public.

The Managing Director is Bob Wallis and Joan Brookes is the Accountant. You are employed as an Accounting Technician to assist Joan Brookes.

DATA

The following transactions all occurred on 1 June 20X3 and have been entered for you into summarised books of original entry. (VAT has in this instance been calculated to the nearest £.)

Treat 'other customers' and 'other suppliers' as individual accounts.

SALES DAY BOOK

	Total £	VAT £	Net £
All Electrical Ltd	3,108	463	2,645
Electromart	2,142	319	1,823
Denman Stores	5,071	755	4,316
Homecare Ltd	1,485	221	1,264
Other customers	14,839	2,210	12,629
	26,645	3,968	22,677

PURCHASES DAY BOOK

	Total £	VAT £	Net £	Goods for resale £	Telephones £
Johnson Imports Ltd	12,518	1,864	10,654	10,654	
Hammond & Co	10,234	1,524	8,710	8,710	
Telecom	870	130	740		740
Other suppliers	2,652	395	2,257	2,257	
	26,274	3,913	22,361	21,621	740

SALES RETURNS DAY BOOK

	Total £	VAT £	Net £
Electromart	99	15	84

PURCHASES RETURNS DAY BOOK

	Total £	VAT £	Net £
Hammond & Co	242	36	206

JOURNAL

DEBIT	Bad debts	£131	
CREDIT	Debtors control account		£131
	Dailey Electrics (included in the balance of other customers) written off (VAT is ignored)		
DEBIT	Postal expenses	£20	
CREDIT	Telephones		£20
	Correction of an error made 25 April 20X3		

CASH BOOK

			£	
Opening balance at start of day			1,491	(debit)

Receipts		Discount £	Net receipt £	
Electromart		84	4,126	
Denman Stores		60	2,958	
			7,084	
			8,575	

Payments	Cheque No	Discount £	Net payment £	
Hammond & Co	000416	75	3,683	
			3,683	
Closing balance at the end of day			4,892	(debit)

The following are *selected balances only* at the start of the day on 1 June 20X3.

Customers	£
All Electrical Ltd	8,312
Electromart	7,966
Denman Stores	5,487
Homecare Ltd	9,523
Other customers	367,844

Suppliers	
Johnson Imports Ltd	26,972
Hammond & Co	18,403
Telecom	NIL
Other suppliers	253,046

Other	
Purchases	1,536,772
Sales	2,003,293
Sales returns	3,941
Purchases returns	2,417
Telephones	623
VAT (credit balance)	32,621
Debtors control account	399,132
Creditors control account	298,421

Task 1

Enter the opening balances into the following accounts.

(a) Debtors control account
(b) Creditors control account
(c) Telephones
(d) Sales
(e) VAT

(f) Electromart
(g) Hammond & Co

These accounts can be found on pages 264 and 265.

Task 2

Enter all relevant transactions into the accounts shown in Task 1.

Task 3

Balance off all the accounts in which you have made entries in Task 2.

Task 4

Calculate the closing balances of the remaining customer accounts and complete the list of balances on Page 266.

Task 5

Calculate the closing balances of the remaining supplier accounts and complete the list of balances on page 266.

Task 6

Reconcile the closing balance of the debtors control account to the total of the list of closing customer balances prepared in Task 4.

Task 7

Reconcile the closing balance of the creditors control account to the total of the list of closing supplier balances prepared in Task 5.

Notes

(a) It is not a requirement to draw up all the individual customer and supplier accounts in order to calculate the closing balances for Tasks 4 and 5. Candidates may, however, adopt that approach if they wish.

(b) Since only selected balances are available it is not possible to check the total of the debit balances against the total of the credit balances.

General ledger

DEBTORS CONTROL ACCOUNT

CREDITORS CONTROL ACCOUNT

TELEPHONES

SALES

VAT

Debtors ledger

ELECTROMART

Creditors ledger

HAMMOND & CO

Control account reconciliations

	£	£
Updated debtors control account balance		
Updated customer balances:		
All Electrical Ltd		
Electromart		
Denman Stores		
Homecare Ltd		
Other customers		
Total updated customer balances		
	£	£
Updated creditors control account balance		
Updated supplier balances:		
Johnson Imports Ltd		
Hammond & Co		
Telecom		
Other suppliers		
Total updated supplier balances		

Lecturers' practice devolved assessment
2 Hairdressing Supplies

Performance criteria

The following performance criteria are covered in this Devolved Assessment.

Element 3.2 Prepare ledger balances and control accounts

1. Relevant accounts are totalled
2. Control accounts are reconciled with the totals of the balance in the subsidiary ledger where appropriate
3. Authorised adjustments are correctly processed and documented

Element 3.3 Draft an initial trial balance

1. Information required for the initial trial balance is identified and obtained from the relevant sources
3. The draft initial trial balance is prepared in line with the organisation's policies and procedures.

Notes on completing the Assessment

This Assessment is designed to test your ability to post transactions correctly to the ledgers, perform a control account reconciliation and prepare an initial trial balance.

You are allowed 2 hours to complete your work.

A high level of accuracy is required. Check your work carefully.

Correcting fluid may be used but should be used in moderation. Errors should be crossed out neatly and clearly. You should write in black ink and not in pencil.

A full answer to this Assessment is provided in the Lecturers' Resource Pack for Unit 3.

Hairdressing Supplies

The seven tasks below are all based on the transactions of Hairdressing Supplies Ltd, a medium-sized wholesaler supplying equipment and other requirements to the hairdressing trade in South East England.

Norman Floater is the managing director, and Marjorie Thistlethwaite the accountant and company secretary. Marjorie is assisted by accounting technician Chris Pollard (yourself) and another office clerk Phylis Cranborne. A manual accounting system is currently operated by the company.

You are required to post to the appropriate ledger accounts from summaries of transactions, (a) to (f) below, for the month of March, the third month of the company's financial year.

At 1 March the balances in the general ledger, the debtors (or sales) ledger, and the creditors (or purchase) ledger are as shown in the accounts in the following ledgers (see pages 270 to 276).

Treat 'Other customers' and 'Other suppliers' as individual accounts.

Work in whole £'s. Your work should be neat, legible and accurate.

DATA

(a) *Credit sales for March*

	Total £	VAT £	Net £
Tony's Salon Ltd	696	104	592
Jean Crane & Co	399	59	340
Euro-Hair Style Ltd	811	121	690
Other customers	48,216	7,181	41,035
	50,122	7,465	42,657

(b) *Credit purchases for March*

	Total £	VAT £	Net £	Goods for resale £	Other items £
International Toiletries	6,367	948	5,419	5,419	
Tonsa Supplies	4,960	739	4,221	4,221	
Short & Long	2,314	345	1,969	1,969	
Other suppliers	16,432	2,447	13,985	9,475	4,510
	30,073	4,479	25,594	21,084	4,510

Analysis of other items purchased

	£
Telephones	630
Advertising	1,011
Postages and stationery	529
Vehicle running expenses	340
Other expenditure	2,000
	4,510

(c) *Returns by customers during March (including VAT @ 17.5%)*

	Total £	VAT £	Net £
Jean Crane & Co	35	5	30
Other customers	141	21	120
	176	26	150

(d) *Returns to suppliers during March (including VAT @ 17.5%)*

	Total £	VAT £	Net £
Other suppliers	115	17	98

(e) *Bank current account for March*

1 March opening balance £36,269 (debit)

Receipts	Cash discount £	Net amount received £
Tony's Salon Ltd		483
Jean Crane & Co		412
Euro-Hair Style Ltd	18	502
Newshorn Wigs plc		279
Other customers	113	38,481
	131	40,157

Payments	Cash discount £	Net amount paid £
International Toiletries		4,521
Tonsa Supplies Ltd	97	3,795
Short & Long plc		2,687
Other suppliers	149	15,819
	246	26,822
Wages and salaries: March		10,168
Customs & Excise: VAT		8,957
Petty cash		43
	246	45,990

(f) *Petty cash summary: March*

	VAT £	Net £	£
Balance at 1 March			23
Reimbursed from bank account			43
			66
Payments			
Postage		12	
Vehicle running expenses	3	19	
Other expenditure	2	16	
	5	47	
			52
Balance at 31 March			14

Task 1

Enter the credit sales (a) and credit purchases (b) into the appropriate ledger accounts.

Task 2

Enter the sales returns (c) and purchase returns (d) into the appropriate ledger accounts.

Task 3

Enter the bank receipts and payments from the bank current account (e) into the other ledger accounts concerned.

Task 4

Enter the petty cash payments from the petty cash summary (f) into the other ledger accounts concerned.

Task 5

Balance off all accounts in the debtors and creditors ledgers, and bring forward the balances at 1 April.

Task 6

Balance off all the accounts in the general ledger at 31 March, except those where there are no new entries during March. Where there are entries on only one side of an account, you need only draw a single line on that side and show the new balance at 31 March as a sub-total. Otherwise balance the accounts and bring forward the balances to 1 April.

Task 7

A list of general ledger account headings is attached (see page 276). Enter all balances at 1 April, including the bank and petty cash balances. Total the two columns. They should agree, but leave the work incomplete if you are unable to trace the errors within the time you have allowed for the exercise.

Debtors ledger

TONY'S SALON LTD

Date	Details	£	Date	Details	£
1 March	Balance b/d	491			

JEAN CRANE & CO

Date	Details	£	Date	Details	£
1 March	Balance b/d	430			

EURO HAIR STYLE LTD

Date	Details	£	Date	Details	£
			1 March	Balance b/d	92

NEWSHORN WIGS PLC

Date	Details	£	Date	Details	£
1 March	Balance b/d	356			

OTHER CUSTOMERS

Date	Details	£	Date	Details	£
1 March	Balance b/d	39,416			

Creditors ledger

INTERNATIONAL TOILETRIES

Date	Details	£	Date	Details	£
			1 March	Balance b/d	4,521

TONSA SUPPLIES LTD

Date	Details	£	Date	Details	£
			1 March	Balance b/d	3,892

SHORT & LONG PLC

Date	Details	£	Date	Details	£
			1 March	Balance b/d	3,104

OTHER SUPPLIERS

Date	Details	£	Date	Details	£
			1 March	Balance b/d	10,783

General ledger

SALES

Date	Details	£	Date	Details	£
			1 March	Balance b/d	101,975

SALES RETURNS

Date	Details	£	Date	Details	£
1 March	Balance b/d	248			

PURCHASES

Date	Details	£	Date	Details	£
1 March	Balance b/d	63,085			

PURCHASE RETURNS

Date	Details	£	Date	Details	£
			1 March	Balance b/d	114

DEBTORS CONTROL ACCOUNT

Date	Details	£	Date	Details	£
1 March	Balance b/d	40,693	1 March	Balance b/d	92

CREDITORS CONTROL ACCOUNT

Date	Details	£	Date	Details	£
			1 March	Balance b/d	22,300

VAT ACCOUNT

Date	Details	£	Date	Details	£
			1 March	Balance b/d	17,994

DISCOUNT ALLOWED

Date	Details	£	Date	Details	£
1 March	Balance b/d	330			

DISCOUNT RECEIVED

Date	Details	£	Date	Details	£
			1 March	Balance b/d	627

STOCK

Date	Details	£	Date	Details	£
1 March	Balance b/d	41,572			

WAGES AND SALARIES

Date	Details	£	Date	Details	£
1 March	Balance b/d	23,127			

POSTAGE AND STATIONERY

Date	Details	£	Date	Details	£
1 March	Balance b/d	1,386			

VEHICLE RUNNING EXPENSES

Date	Details	£	Date	Details	£
1 March	Balance b/d	841			

OTHER EXPENDITURE

Date	Details	£	Date	Details	£
1 March	Balance b/d	3,813			

TELEPHONES

Date	Details	£	Date	Details	£

ADVERTISING

Date	Details	£	Date	Details	£
1 March	Balance b/d	775			

FIXED ASSETS

Date	Details	£	Date	Details	£
1 March	Balance b/d	190,500			

CAPITAL

Date	Details	£	Date	Details	£
			1 March	Balance b/d	259,560

General ledger balances at 31 March

	Debit £	Credit £
Sales		
Sales returns		
Purchases		
Purchase returns		
Debtors control account		
Creditors control account		
VAT		
Discount allowed		
Discount received		
Stock		
Wages and salaries		
Postage and stationery		
Vehicle running expenses		
Other expenditure		
Telephones		
Advertising		
Fixed assets		
Capital and reserves		
Cash at bank		
Petty cash		
Totals		

Lecturers' practice central assessment

LECTURERS' PRACTICE CENTRAL ASSESSMENT

FOUNDATION STAGE
REVISED STANDARDS
NVQ/SVQ LEVEL 2 IN ACCOUNTING

Preparing Ledger Balances and an Initial Trial Balance

The Central Assessment is in two parts.

Section 1   Processing Exercise
Complete all 5 tasks

Section 2   Ten Tasks and Questions
Complete all tasks and questions

DO NOT OPEN THIS PAPER UNTIL YOU ARE READY TO START UNDER TIMED CONDITIONS

Lecturers' practice central assessment

You are reminded that competence must be achieved in each section You should therefore attempt and aim to complete EVERY task in BOTH sections. All essential workings should be included within your answers where appropriate

You are advised to spend 90 minutes on Section 1 and 90 minutes on Section 2.

INTRODUCTION

The tasks and questions are based on the transactions of Summit Glazing Ltd. The company provides a glazing service to commercial and domestic customers. It also constructs conservatories and installs replacement windows which are bought in from specialist manufacturers.

The Managing Director is Chris Cooper and Mary Owen is the Accountant/Company Secretary. You are employed as an Accounting Technician to assist Mary Owen.

DATA

The following transactions all occurred on 1 December 20X5 and have yet to be entered into the ledger system. VAT has been calculated at the rate of 17.5%.

Sales invoices issued

	Total £	VAT £	Net £
GCJ Builders Ltd	8,460	1,260	7,200
Acorn Housing Association	6,063	903	5,160
Cordington plc	2,021	301	1,720
James Building Services	799	119	680
	17,343	2,583	14,760

Purchases invoices received

	Total £	VAT £	Net £
Georgian Conservatories	705	105	600
Diamond Glass Ltd	2,115	315	1,800
Russell Timber Supplies	423	63	360
Elite Windows	1,269	189	1,080
	4,512	672	3,840

Credit note received

	Total £	VAT £	Net £
Diamond Glass Ltd	47	7	40

Cash sales

	Total £	VAT £	Net £
Cheques	141	21	120
Notes and coins	188	28	160
	329	49	280

Cheque received

	£
Acorn Housing Association	6,200

Cheques issued

	£
Georgian Conservatories	27,195
(Full settlement of a debt of £27,750)	
Elite Windows	13,995

Journal Entry

	Debit £	Credit £
Motor expenses	340	
Motor vehicles		340

Correction of error: cost of repairs on delivery van debited in error to the motor vehicles account.

Opening balances

The following balances are available to you at the start of the day on 1 December 20X5.

	£
Purchases	897,953
Sales	1,138,325
Purchase returns	4,280
Bank (debit balance)	22,723
Bank charges	1,567
VAT (credit balance)	8,136
Discounts allowed	6,340
Discounts received	2,892
Sales ledger control (debtors)	85,995
Purchase ledger control (creditors)	78,237
Wages	282,500
Rent and rates	16,225
Electricity	4,106
Telephone	1,852
Motor expenses	6,857
Insurance	5,935
Sundry expenses	2,734
Motor vehicles	56,900
Machinery and equipment	15,120
Sundry creditors	11,867
Stocks	48,930
Capital	212,000

SECTION 1 - PROCESSING EXERCISE (Suggested time allocation: 90 minutes)

COMPLETE ALL THE FOLLOWING TASKS

Task 1 Enter the opening balances into the following accounts:

> Bank (cash book)
> Sales ledger control (debtors)
> Purchase ledger control (creditors)
> Purchases
> Sales
> VAT
> Purchase returns
> Discounts received
> Motor vehicles
> Motor expenses

These accounts can be found on pages 283 to 286

Task 2 Using the data shown on pages 280 and 281, enter all the transactions into the accounts given in Task 1.

Task 3 Balance the cash book and total the discount and VAT columns, transferring the totals to the appropriate accounts.

Task 4 Balance all the remaining accounts in which you have made entries.

Note. You are not required to update any accounts other than those shown in Task 1.

Task 5 Complete the trial balance on page 287 by inserting the figure for each account in either the debit column or the credit column as appropriate. Total the two columns. The two totals should be the same. If they do not agree, try to trace and correct any errors you have made within the time available. If you are still unable to make the totals balance, leave the work incomplete.

MAIN LEDGER

Sales Ledger Control

Date	Details	Amount £	Date	Details	Amount £

Purchase Ledger Control

Date	Details	Amount £	Date	Details	Amount £

Purchases

Date	Details	Amount £	Date	Details	Amount £

Sales

Date	Details	Amount	Date	Details	Amount
		£			£

VAT

Date	Details	Amount	Date	Details	Amount
		£			£

Purchase Returns

Date	Details	Amount	Date	Details	Amount
		£			£

Discounts Received

Date	Details	Amount	Date	Details	Amount
		£			£

Motor Vehicles

Date	Details	Amount	Date	Details	Amount
		£			£

Motor Expenses

Date	Details	Amount	Date	Details	Amount
		£			£

Lecturers' practice central assessment

CASH BOOK

Date	Details	Discount allowed	VAT	Cash	Bank	Date	Details	Discount received	VAT	Cash	Bank

UPDATED TRIAL BALANCE

	Debit balances £	Credit balances £
Purchases	....	....
Sales	....	....
Purchase returns	....	....
Bank	....	....
Bank charges	....	....
Cash	....	....
VAT	....	....
Discounts allowed	....	....
Discounts received	....	....
Sales ledger control (debtors)	....	....
Purchase ledger control (creditors)	....	....
Wages	....	....
Rent and rates	....	....
Electricity	....	....
Telephone	....	....
Motor expenses	....	....
Insurance	....	....
Sundry expenses	....	....
Motor vehicles	....	....
Machinery and equipment	....	....
Sundry creditors	....	....
Stocks	....	....
Capital	....	....
Totals	_____	_____

SECTION 2: TASKS AND QUESTIONS (Suggested time allocation: 90 minutes)

Using where appropriate, the information given in Section 1, write in the space provided *or* circle the correct answer. Do *not* indicate your choice in any other way. Answer *all* the following questions.

1

```
National Bank plc                    27 November 20X4
82 Market Street Swindon

Pay    Summit Glazing Limited
       Five hundred and four pounds / ACCOUNT PAYEE /    £ 540.00
                                                            C Lawton
```

The above cheque has been received from a customer. Give two reasons why it would not be accepted for payment if it was presented to National Bank plc.

(a) ....

(b) ....

2 What bookkeeping entries are required in the general ledger to record a dishonoured cheque which has been received from a customer and paid into Summit Glazing's bank account.

(a) Debit..

(b) Credit...

3 Summit Glazing Ltd are planning to purchase a new van. Would the following items be capital or revenue expenditure?

(a) The purchase price of the van

Capital / Revenue

(b) Modification work to the side of the van to allow the external carriage of sheets of glass

Capital / Revenue

(c) Motor insurance for the van

Capital / Revenue

4 Complete the following sentences by inserting the name of the appropriate document.

(a) Summit Glazing sends out a ....to each credit customer on a monthly basis which summarises the transactions that have taken place and shows the amount owed by the customer.

(b) Summit Glazing sends out a .... to a credit customer in order to correct an error where the customer has been overcharged by an invoice.

(c) Summit Glazing sends out a .... with a payment to a supplier to indicate which invoices are being paid.

5 Classify the following ledger accounts according to whether they represent asset/liability/expense or revenue.

(a) Insurance

Asset / Liability / Expense / Revenue

(b) Stock

Asset / Liability / Expense / Revenue

(c) Discounts received

Asset / Liability / Expense / Revenue

(d) Bank overdraft

Asset / Liability / Expense / Revenue

6 During the quarter ended 31 October 20X5, sales amounted to £731,555 inclusive of VAT at 17.5%. On the 31 October the credit balance on the VAT account was £47,600. Calculate the value of vatable purchases made during the quarter *inclusive* of VAT.

Note. Your answer should include detailed workings.

....
....
....

7 What bookkeeping entries would be necessary to record a cash refund of £94 (inclusive of VAT) to a customer?

Debit	Amount £	Credit	Amount £
....	....	....	....
....	....	....	....

8 Would the following errors cause a difference between the balance of the purchase ledger (creditors) control account and the total of the balances in the purchase ledger?

(a) The purchase day book was overcast by £10.

Yes / No

(b) The value of a purchase invoice was credited to the account of ACL Ltd instead of A C Lead Ltd.

Yes / No

(c) An invoice for £47 was recorded in the purchase day book as £74.

Yes / No

9   Would the following errors cause a difference to occur between the balance of the creditors control account and the total of the balances in the purchases ledger?

    (a) A creditor's account has been balanced off incorrectly.

    Yes / No

    (b) An invoice for £37 has been entered into the purchases day book as £39.

    Yes / No

    (c) An invoice has, in error, been omitted from the purchases day book.

    Yes / No

10 A manufacturer sells a product to a wholesaler for £200 plus VAT of £35. The wholesaler sells the same product to a retailer for £280 plus VAT of £49. The retailer then sells the product to a customer for £320 plus VAT of £56. What is the total amount of VAT collectable by HM Customs & Excise relating to the product?

    £........................

ROUGH WORK

See overleaf for information on other
BPP products and how to order

AAT Order

To BPP Publishing Ltd, Aldine Place, London W12 8AW
Tel: 020 8740 2211. Fax: 020 8740 1184
E-mail: Publishing@bpp.com Web: www.bpp.com

Mr/Mrs/Ms (Full name) _____

Daytime delivery address _____

Postcode _____

Daytime Tel _____

E-mail _____

	5/01 Texts	6/01 Kits	5/01 Passcards	Tapes	Special offer
FOUNDATION (ALL £9.95)					
Unit 1 Recording Income and Receipts	☐	☐	☐		All Foundation Texts and Kits (£80) ☐
Unit 2 Making and Recording Payments	☐	☐	☐		
Unit 3 Ledger Balances and Initial Trial Balance	☐	☐	£4.95 ☐	£10.00 ☐	
Unit 4 Supplying Information for Mgmt Control	☐	☐	☐		
Unit 20 Working with Information Technology	☐	☐	☐		
Unit 22/23 Healthy Workplace & Personal Effectiveness	☐	☐			
INTERMEDIATE (ALL £9.95)		8/01 Kits			
Unit 5 Financial Records and Accounts	☐	☐	£4.95 ☐	£10.00 ☐	All Inter'te Texts and Kits (£65) ☐
Unit 6 Cost Information	☐	☐	£4.95 ☐	£10.00 ☐	
Unit 7 Reports and Returns	☐	☐			
Unit 21 Using Information Technology	☐	☐			
TECHNICIAN (ALL £9.95)					
Unit 8/9 Core Managing Costs and Allocating Resources	☐	☐	£4.95 ☐	£10.00 ☐	Set of 12 Technician Texts/Kits (Please specify titles required) (£100) ☐
Unit 10 Core Managing Accounting Systems	☐	☐			
Unit 11 Option Financial Statements (A/c Practice)	☐	☐	£4.95 ☐	£10.00 ☐	
Unit 12 Option Financial Statements (Central Govnmt)	☐	☐			
Unit 15 Option Cash Management and Credit Control	☐	☐			
Unit 16 Option Evaluating Activities	☐	☐			
Unit 17 Option Implementing Auditing Procedures	☐	☐			
Unit 18 Option Business Tax (FA01)(8/01 Text)	☐				
Unit 19 Option Personal Tax (FA 01)(8/01 Text)	☐				
TECHNICIAN 2000 (ALL £9.95)					
Unit 18 Option Business Tax FA00 (8/00 Text & Kit)	☐				
Unit 19 Option Personal Tax FA00 (8/00 Text & Kit)	☐				
SUBTOTAL	£	£	£	£	£

TOTAL FOR PRODUCTS £ _____

POSTAGE & PACKING

Texts/Kits
	First	Each extra
UK (max £10)	£2.00	£2.00
Europe*	£4.00	£2.00
Rest of world	£20.00	£10.00

Passcards/Tapes
	First	Each extra
UK	£2.00	£1.00
Europe*	£2.50	£1.00
Rest of world	£15.00	£8.00

Grand Total (Cheques to *BPP Publishing*) I enclose a cheque for (incl. Postage) £ _____

Or charge to Access/Visa/Switch

Card Number ☐☐☐☐ ☐☐☐☐ ☐☐☐☐ ☐☐☐☐

Expiry date _____ Start Date _____

Issue Number (Switch Only) _____

Signature _____

We aim to deliver to all UK addresses inside 5 working days; a signature will be required. Orders to all EU addresses should be delivered within 6 working days. All other orders to overseas addresses should be delivered within 8 working days. * Europe includes the Republic of Ireland and the Channel Islands.

AAT - Unit 3 Ledger Balances and Initial Trial Balance Assessment Kit (6/01)

REVIEW FORM & FREE PRIZE DRAW

All original review forms from the entire BPP range, completed with genuine comments, will be entered into one of two draws on 31 January 2002 and 31 July 2002. The names on the first four forms picked out on each occasion will be sent a cheque for £50.

Name: _____   Address: _____
_____
_____

How have you used this Assessment Kit?
(Tick one box only)
☐ Home study (book only)
☐ On a course: college _____
☐ With 'correspondence' package
☐ Other _____

Why did you decide to purchase this Devolved Assessment Kit? *(Tick one box only)*
☐ Have used BPP Texts in the past
☐ Recommendation by friend/colleague
☐ Recommendation by a lecturer at college
☐ Saw advertising
☐ Other _____

During the past six months do you recall seeing/receiving any of the following?
(Tick as many boxes as are relevant)
☐ Our advertisement in *Accounting Technician* magazine
☐ Our advertisement in *Pass*
☐ Our brochure with a letter through the post

Which (if any) aspects of our advertising do you find useful?
(Tick as many boxes as are relevant)
☐ Prices and publication dates of new editions
☐ Information on Interactive Text content
☐ Facility to order books off-the-page
☐ None of the above

Have you used the companion Interactive Text for this subject?   ☐ Yes   ☐ No

Your ratings, comments and suggestions would be appreciated on the following areas

	Very useful	Useful	Not useful
Introductory section (How to use this Assessment Kit etc)	☐	☐	☐
Practice activities	☐	☐	☐
Practice devolved assessments	☐	☐	☐
Trial run devolved assessment	☐	☐	☐
AAT Sample simulation	☐	☐	☐
Trial run central assessments	☐	☐	☐
AAT central assessments	☐	☐	☐
Lecturers' Resource Pack activities	☐	☐	☐
Content of answers	☐	☐	☐
Layout of pages	☐	☐	☐
Structure of book and ease of use	☐	☐	☐

	Excellent	Good	Adequate	Poor
Overall opinion of this Kit	☐	☐	☐	☐

Do you intend to continue using BPP Assessment Kits/Interactive Texts/?   ☐ Yes   ☐ No

Please note any further comments and suggestions/errors on the reverse of this page.

Please return to: Nick Weller, BPP Publishing Ltd, FREEPOST, London, W12 8BR

REVIEW FORM & FREE PRIZE DRAW (continued)

Please note any further comments and suggestions/errors below

FREE PRIZE DRAW RULES

1. Closing date for 31 January 2002 draw is 31 December 2001. Closing date for 31 July 2002 draw is 30 June 2002.
2. Restricted to entries with UK and Eire addresses only. BPP employees, their families and business associates are excluded.
3. No purchase necessary. Entry forms are available upon request from BPP Publishing. No more than one entry per title, per person. Draw restricted to persons aged 16 and over.
4. Winners will be notified by post and receive their cheques not later than 6 weeks after the relevant draw date.
5. The decision of the promoter in all matters is final and binding. No correspondence will be entered into.